Shekinah
שכינה

The Word of God

Kelly SEBASTINA

John 1:1 - In the beginning was ~~The Word~~ **Shekinah**, and ~~The Word~~ **Shekinah** was with God, and ~~The Word~~ **Shekinah** was God.

'John was writing in Greek. There was no Greek equivalent for **Shekinah**, which Jews were careful to distinguish from the utterly transcendent reality of God itself.'

Karen ARMSTRONG

Pg 160, Jerusalem: One City, Three Faiths
1996, Ballantyne

Copyright © 2014 Kelly SEBASTINA

All rights reserved.

ISBN-13: 978-1493747429

ISBN-10: 1493747428

FOR RENÉE

CONTENTS

I - Piercing The Veil 7
  1 Teen-Nymph 9
  2 Escape Velocity 14
  3 Finn MacCool 19
  4 Sweet Little Lies 28
  5 Zombie 34
  6 Sacred Grove 40
  7 Supernova 43
  8 In Thru' The Out Door 48
  9 Anaconda 52
  10 Shekinah 58
  11 The Long Goodbye 61

II - Riding The Snake 67
  1 La Flaqueza Del Bolchevique 69
  2 Sofia 75
  3 Train Kept a Rollin' 80
  4 Cougar 85
  5 Isis 92

III - Nectar of Immortality 99
  1 Michael Douglas 101
  2 Mojo 107
  3 Selket 111
  4 Shape Shifting Goddess 116
  5 Asherah 119

I - PIERCING THE VEIL

Kelly SEBASTINA

The Setting - Our story opens in an apartment in Lisboa, under a wintry morning sun, where Angie; a perky, bright and preconscious teen; is getting ready to meet someone special, watched with a helpless scowl by her eagle-eyed mother.

1 - TEEN-NYMPH

Angie; Angie, short for Angela, was excited; Chris was due to arrive today. Angie was 19, brilliant, top of her class, looked hot, accounts major, loved, adored and desired by every pimpled idiot within a radius of a 100 nautical miles.

The reason for her excitement was Chris; though her mother (stupidly) preferred she call him 'Uncle Chris'. Not only because he happened to be Uncle Joãozinho's brother; who was married to Aunt Gabriela, her mother's youngest sister; but also because she (stupidly) thought the fig leaf of respectability may stop her heart from slamming against her ribs every time she thought of him.

So what was the big deal? The big deal was that he lived in Brasília and came up for a couple of weeks a year for one of those typical family reunions; filled with kids, noise, presents, the usual racket - on Christmas holiday. These were typical full-house affairs, guaranteeing no-intimacy, or in other words, no chance to tell him how she felt or, more importantly, WHAT she felt. It bothered her, had done more so since the past 5 years, when she was 14 when 'it' happened.

She remembered the incident, which marked a change in their relationship; she was 14 and was larking about as usual; like a typical stupid teen, dressed in Tees and skimpy shorts when she spied him and jumped onto his lap; as she always did, wherever she found him. This time was different though; her parents had exchanged disapproving glances; her mother had a weird look on her face; she sensed a sudden chill in the atmosphere, and that was the end of it.

They watched her like hawks now, especially her mother, more so when HE was around. She hadn't known why, then, but she knew now. The eagle-eyed looks didn't bother her, she didn't lose sleep over that, but over what she'd felt for the first time.

Coming back to the incident, something even strange followed which puzzled her, though he - cool as cucumber, had slipped her off and said, 'C'mon Baby, let's have an ice', and got up to walk away.

She'd love it when he spoke to her like that, it was intimate, the way he'd call her his 'Baby' or 'Sweetheart', even when her mom was around.

The incident had imprinted itself in her memory and she'd analysed it a million times. She knew things had changed, but exactly what and why she couldn't say. She'd suddenly started feeling shy, which was quite out of character for her, and freaked out because she didn't know why.

Or did she? As a rule, she never lied to herself and that meant did she know the answer only too well? She was, now, conscious of his presence - a touch, a glance, a peck on the cheek had multiple undertones; she no longer felt as confident of her feelings. She was unsteady and unsure was it just 'puppy love' or . . . something else? Screw it!!! Suffice it to say she hadn't been the same since then.

What irritated her no end was that her mother's curiosity had been aroused. She'd started to pry, check her cell, as if she thought she wouldn't find out; she'd pop-in suddenly to conduct surprise checks when HE was around; stammer weak reasons to stop her going out with HIM, especially alone, even for ice-cream; and more and more stuff like that. Anyway, who was worried? Not her, no way. Her parents lived on another freakin' planet for all she cared.

There was a glimmer of understanding as she grew up and her body developed. She recalled her best friend Cintia's glance of approval, 'You've got a terrific butt, on top of sculpted calves . . . dangerous.'

She was secretly pleased. She knew she was hot, though her breasts could be bigger plus she could be fairer. Her mother said she had Moorish blood which was belied by the red tinge to her hair and a reddish tan to her skin. Plus, her face went red when she was angry or just plain impatient. Did that also explain her hot-temper, passionate nature and razor sharp brain??? She didn't know, would ask Chris.

Another incident, she recalled, on one of these reunions, he'd taken everyone out for dinner. She'd carefully sidled next to him on the walk home so that their shoulders occasionally touched and her hand 'accidentally' met his. Their fingers had entwined, and, what pleased her no end; as if it was perfectly natural; he hadn't pulled away but continued to hold her perspiring little palm.

It was also the first time she felt 'something'; not her heart, which thudded violently against her chest, not the hairs at the nape of her neck, stiff with anticipation. It was more 'down there', virgin territory, her jeans had felt tighter than usual, there was a sudden dampness, perhaps, didn't know why or maybe she did but wouldn't admit . . .Great stuff witch, now you've started to lie to yourself as well.

That short walk home was etched in her brain. She

knew, since then, it was only a matter of time before 'it' happened. The thought made her mouth dry, she almost fainted; her knees trembled with excitement and her cheeks burnt with shame. Nice Catholic girls don't think these things, her mother would say.

Don't worry, she quickly forgave herself, it was all make-believe anyway, a product of a teen-crush, begun an awful long time ago. Her friends envied her, took care to remind her that it was a one-sided affair and it wouldn't work. Screw them – they didn't bother her - if you were in love; even if the only one; you were in love.

Flashback to the second time - she was in his room, looking for something to read, he'd come up from the back, hugged her tight, spontaneously, like he'd always do, and bent to kiss her cheek. She turned in the nick of time, to catch him on the mouth, a spray of sea-salt merged with his after-shave; Gillette, Pacific Light, non-alcoholic, Boston MA 02199; see the extent of her madness, she'd stolen one, kept it in her wardrobe, used it when she . . . her ears again burnt hot with shame. His stubble was like heaven, time froze, somewhere her mom shrieked, he'd let go with a strange expression on his face, she knew then that something had clicked - it was a 'tell.'

The third occasion was last year. This time she was older, wiser, more experienced - lying witch – Okay, in theory at least, checking out www.xnxx.com on her laptop had 'educated' her on what nice Catholic girls didn't do, hee hee ^_^

Also, she was not as jumpy, as earlier. They were sprawled over the carpet, checking out a movie in the living room, some of them asleep, the others drowsy with exhaustion but not keen on going to bed.

The lights were dimmed. She moved her 'sculpted' calves, as Cintia called them, to rest over his hand, her pulse had raced but she kept her cool. He pretended (how did she know?) not to notice and didn't move; neither did she; until her mother came, as if on cue, to yank her in.

2 - ESCAPE VELOCITY

Phew ... Chris was here at last and she was dumb if she'd leave it at that.

'Now where . . .?' her mother bleated.

'I'm staying over at Aunt Rita's'; she cut-in before she could finish.

'Why?'

'Uncle Chris is here, Mumma, you know I always do that.'

A scowl, 'How will you go?'

'Like I always do; a tram to Parque das Nações and then the number 49; c'mon Mamma, I've done it before.'

'But. . . but . . .', her mother had a hand on her heart, the other half-heartedly perched on the door-latch.

What did the witch think? That she could stop her? Anyway, she knew what to do – in a well practiced move, she dug her nails in her mothers forearm, ripped her upper skin off, while she simultaneously pulled open the door with the other.

She was out in a flash; her mother's scream followed in her wake, 'Pouco vagabunda! Desova do diabo!' (Little slut! Spawn of the Devil!)

She giggled as she sped down the stairs and heard her plaintive wail, 'I'll come to get you tomorrow.'

'Yeah, sure,' Angie thought with a frown, 'you and who else witch.'

She remembered the kids, stopped at the Store; filled her satchel with chewing-gum, candy and coke - a staple diet for every toddler.

The tram arrived and after a brief stop, she was finally on her way. Why oh why did it take so long, thick weekend traffic, more delays, the speed agonisingly slow, did time move differently for lovers? What was that again, witch? Lovers! She knew she was going insane; to live continuously in a childhood fantasy dream-world was proof that she'd finally lost it.

To get off the topic, she checked her cell. There were the usual assortment of missed calls and messages. She deleted the ones from losers, and jumped when she saw a text from him – how did he know? She hadn't told him, she wanted to take him by surprise. It must have been her mother, who'd have called Aunt Rita, and who would've spilled the beans.

In any event, his text read: 'Baby, why rush it, we cd hv met 2morrow?'

'Can't wait Uncle, hv 2 c u now.' She smirked. She wanted to add, 'u kno' why' but didn't.

'Same here Sweetheart.'

She promptly saved it under another name since her mother routinely checked her texts, especially after she'd confiscated her Maria CAPRIO collection; and all this in a country where the age of consent was 16.

Move, please, faster, can't you? The impersonal cosmopolitan traffic had a will of its own; another tram-stop, another wait. She suddenly noticed glances of approval from guys – teens, bikers, adults; she looked good and she knew it.

'Sorry jerks, you're nowhere near his class,' she thought with a smile.

To pass the time, she texted Cintia: 'D'u think it cd happen 2nite?'

'No Angie, it doesn't work out that way.'

She was irritated; screw her, who cares what she thought. Cintia had done it at 17, with a loser who promptly dumped her after the event. Or non-event. It was her fault as well; you didn't have to be a magician to make your boyfriend disappear. A trip to the honey-grove did the trick.

Anyway, getting into bed wasn't the problem. Angie knew she could too, but her heart was booked, and the heart never lied. Thank Santa Maria, we're on the move. Santa Maria was the Holy Mother for her, and in whom she passionately believed. Regular visits to Her Church at Belém, short for Bethlehem, kept her conscience clean, or at least that's what she thought. 'Forgive me Mother, for what my thoughts are leading me up to, but I can't help it,' she prayed silently.

She'd reached Parque das Nações, and now waited for the Number 49. She wished she'd taken something to read - she was getting impatient. Well, just for something to do, she double-checked her inventory. All okay.

Let's take another dab of Chanel Allure, her last birthday present from him, slip a strip of Listerine POCKETPAKS in her mouth; the burst of mint hit her brain, spiked through her nose; would he like the taste? Wait a minute, what was that witch?

Her hand shook at the implications underlying her thoughts. Why was she so freakin' nervous? What was it this time? Why now? What was going on here? Switch to plain-speak: Did she want him? The shock of her feelings was like a blow, almost physical, it made her mouth dry, her heart raced on, the hair at the nape of her neck tingled - could she still pretend? Who was she kidding?

She was angry at herself, look somewhere else to shift the blame. Yeah, it was all his fault - for one, why was he the freakin' Sphinx? That's right, she explored it further - If he'd cut her off or even given a hint that he wasn't interested (in THAT sense), she'd have settled down, maybe picked up a boyfriend even, though the thought made her puke. Stop lying, just stop it witch.

Okay she would. Once again, like a dog chasing its tail, her thoughts came back to the same question - Why was it different NOW? Why did her legs press so tightly together, her waist feet tight? There was a tightness between her legs and her breath going shallow.

Why had she selected her tightest pair of jeans today? No accident witch, you want to seduce him. YES, she screamed inside her head, so what?

Phew, she'd admitted it; finally, what was so wrong about that? It's been a freakin' one-sided show till now; she wasn't harming anyone (except herself). There was not even a glimmer of response from him; till yet. Careful, she told herself, her mouth set in a grim straight line; watch where your thoughts are leading to, witch!!!

It was time to disengage, here was the bus. She climbed on, while continuing to dream-on. But what if he rejects you? I'll kill myself, she thought, but would it be any use? Like, would he repent? More importantly, how would she look in a coffin? What would she wear? It wouldn't be jeans and a blouse. Would she look good? Her eyes grew moist at the thought.

Would he show some emotion, finally? Maybe even kiss her lips? The tragedy of the scene brought tears to her eyes.

Should she leave a note, accusing him? Her mother would certainly find it first, no, not if she left it with Cintia, with detailed instructions; she warmed to the theme, the thought kept her occupied for some time.

Naaaaah, this time something would happen. She knew, she though couldn't say why. At times, she scared herself. Should she consult the Holy Mother, maybe ask for a sign or some help perhaps? Was it wrong to desire someone you love? Was she a fool? Did she deliberately make herself irresistible?

No, strike-out the last one; she knew the answer to that. She'd painstakingly worked over-n-over to get bare arms and sexy summer legs, even though her mother howled, 'Catholic girls don't use hair remover till they're married.'

Yeah, sure, stupid, they go around like Grizzly's in the bloom of their youth and worry later why they're spinsters.

One more stop and she'd be there.

3 - FINN MacCOOL

She sped up the incline and finally entered the apartment block. She sighed as she waited for the elevator while the teens, lounging in the yard, checked her out. She knew some of them but didn't have time for 'kids' she thought with a supercilious smile.

Not today anyway. Watch out, one, then two, detached themselves from the group and swaggered her way. Freakin' morons, as if she was interested. Don't Look - Don't Look - Don't Look, keep your eyes glued to the readout, 9, 8, 7, 6, 5, 4, 3, 2, 1, down.

She ran in before the idiots could come any closer and the doors closed. Sorry jerks, my heart and soul are taken, my body remains, tee hee ^_^. She was surprised at herself with her burst of witticism. Maybe she'd write a book about it, but that'd be later, much later.

She'd reached her floor; she got out and pressed the bell.

Thankfully he opened the door and put her out of her misery. She ran into his arms, I don't care, let them stare. No one did in the rush of welcoming her. She was crushed by hugs by visiting Uncles and Aunts Adalina, Rita and

Sara, the pesky kids screaming her name with the small ones going for her legs. She'd got candy for them all, plus gum for the ones with teeth.

'Hi Sweetheart', his tone was light; did she detect a trace of humour?

Don't overreact, she told herself; he held her at arm's length while the kids screamed and snatched her satchel; 'C'mon, let's take a look at my Angel.'

In the wake of her thoughts, it was the wrong thing to say. Her ears burnt hot, she blushed, stammered she-didn't-know-what, thought, 'for god's sake, Witch, WAKE UP. This was so un-professional.

'How are you Chris?' she managed to blurt out, flustered by the attention she'd attracted.

Glares from Aunt Rita, 'Uncle Chris' she warned, her mother must have told her, screw it, she knelt down to hide her shame and grabbed a toddler, squeezing the breath out of him. 'Angie, stop!!!'

The conversation changed, soon it was back to normal, just like old times, the crowd milled about while she got busy helping Aunt Rita in the kitchen.

The men got stuffed, while simultaneously, getting drunk. She wondered why they weren't like Chris, instead of a collection of porcos [pigs]. But why blame them? After all, they lived in a country named after Port Wine but could also be called Porcugal and be equally, if not more, appropriate. The Cock, their National Animal, summarised their National Character rather nicely, didn't you think.

She was grateful that her heartbeat and breathing had returned to normal. She was good at PC i.e. Polite Conversation, answered a few inane questions, about studies, what she planned to do, where she was enrolled and more of the same stupid things grown-ups think teenagers cared about.

Shekinah

The children scampered around, the pre-teens and teens were busy in a world of their own - where gaming devices and play-stations held centre-stage.

Dinner was finally over and she was busy clearing the dishes. Thankfully there was no broken glass this time around. It was late, she'd been on her feet all this while; she took a deep breath and sighed. Phew. He was busy talking; she'd crossed him once or twice; had caught a strange 'look' in his eyes, and the half-smile.

Her thoughts swirled darkly, 'Is he on the same grid?' She was too scared to guess, Oh Holy Mother, stay with me, she prayed weakly.

'Let's go down for a walk', someone said, 'yeah lets', the teens got up, she hesitated, until he said, 'great'; and then they were down for ices and cokes.

They were loud and had loads of fun until it was time to return. They hadn't spoken a word to each other but she was enveloped in a warm cozy feeling. It was the same as before, her thoughts were hazy, the darkness was soothing, comforting, plus something else ^-^!

She knew Cloud-9 existed 'coz she was there. His arm encircled her 26-inch waist, probably to protect her from incoming traffic, he'd loosely pulled her to his side, but this couldn't be the reason. He'd hesitate, pull his arm away when someone looked back, she thought knew, that both were co-conspirators; he would then disengage and pretend to talk shop.

She 'accidently' stumbled against him in the elevator, he didn't notice; or appeared not to. What did it mean? Did he want her? Did he even know what she felt for him? He doesn't drink, so he's sober; then what could the freakin' silence mean? Did she dare hope that she had a chance? The thought made her heart go wonky yet again - no wonder they called it heartache.

'Holy Mother of God, Santa Maria, help me', she thought, was this real or fantasy? Why won't he tell, acknowledge her existence in the way she wanted, not as a freakin' kid. It was agony. She knew she existed only for him.

Her thoughts wandered around to the time when she'd follow him around, all over the place, like a puppy whenever he'd visit. Was she too scared to admit what she really wanted? Maybe she didn't know it herself; no, that she did, she'd fantasised about it even; her cheeks went crimson at the thought; and refused to see. Yes, she was lying to herself. She was a coward and a liar. So what witch? Big freakin' deal.

It was past midnight; the lights, except the ones in the living room, were out. The Aunts - Adalina, Rita and Sara - continued to yak; toys were collected and packed; kids bathed and forced to bed. The grown-ups continued to drink while she drifted away to change.

She had a shower; the needle jets of warm water appeared soothing. She changed and sprayed a hint of Chanel Allure, thought for a second, then peeled off her Aire bra to free her puppies. She'd selected loose Tees because her aunts might notice. She put on her tights, no panties, she'd chosen black, no kidding witch; this was heavy armour, no escape for him this time.

What was that again? Yes, this was deliberate; she was a nocturnal predator on the loose. She was relieved it was out of the closet, she felt excited yet calm. Electricity crackled in the air. Something was bound to happen tonight, she knew that as every fibre of her body crackled with foreknowledge.

The older kids were sprawled over the carpet – some were asleep while some tried their best not to. The teens dozed close to the screen.

'El Laberinto del Fauno ' played at full volume. She was glad of the darkness and sound, did a quick check, felt relieved to have spotted Chris on the carpet. One porco high on vinho, was dead to the world and snored on the couch. The movie played on, no one was interested but neither did they want to sleep. Her arrival went unnoticed, even by him, or did it really?

Fine Chris, it's not my fault, you provoked me, now take this; she pretended to reach for a cushion and glued her chest to his back.

'Okay Finn Mac Cool, let's see you resist that.'

The results were instantaneous and she was elated!!!She felt his heartbeat pound through his 'blades', mmmmm, naughty, naughty, keeping secrets aren't we Uncle Chris?

She sat down, not next to him - that'd be too obvious, and the cows might walk in any minute. She relied on her eyes – they were sharp; like an eagle, or perhaps an owl, in the darkness, on the lookout for any movement. She wished she had night-vision like Seal Team-6, but there was no threat, the aunts were busy catching up on family gossip.

Okay, here goes, it was now or she'd lose her nerve. She slowly extended her legs towards his hand, rested her ankles on his fingers, he didn't withdraw, somehow she knew he wouldn't, but, again, what did it mean?

For some time she stayed the way she was, he appeared to be busy watching the screen, then, what seemed like an eternity later; though she should've anticipated it; his hand casually brushed up her calves.

The movement was unexpected and electric and caught her by surprise. There was a knee jerk reaction as she drew her legs in tighter to keep herself in check. His hand withdrew. Oh no, this was all wrong, she had to do something right away or he'd get the wrong impression.

She did quick check to see if anyone was around. She double checked the freakin' porcos - grunts and drunken snores the only signs of life there, thank goodness for the vinho. The teens were fast asleep, and only the passage lights were on - she'd notice her Aunts shadow before they walked in.

It was now or never, she thought, as she moved closer; and casually held his hand, waited for a while and in a sudden move, pulled it and placed it between her legs while crossing them tight. Was he surprised? Who cared!!!

He glanced aside but she was too frightened to look. She kept her head down while her cheeks burned with shame and her heartbeat and pulse skyrocketed. He was nonchalant, continued to look ahead, but his hand stayed where it was.

Phew, she exhaled, she'd made it, so far so good, it'd been touch-and-go for awhile; at least 'that' was over. She waited for her breath to return to normal. She relaxed and reflected - she'd been scared to death, never again, this hadn't been easy, she could afford to laugh now, she giggled with relief, is this how it was?

Not a word spoken; in any event The Sphinx was freakin' inscrutable; would he do something now or would he need help? She glanced his way, his hand had tensed up, what was he thinking? She dared not hope. Could it be true? Did he want her? Or was he just being polite, thought she was just another stupid teen!

'I'll kill myself, I swear', she was confused. What was it? Was it her call? Should she shouldn't she? Could she be in control? In for a penny, in for a pound, it was heady, what did she have to fear? She was an adult for heaven's sake, a grown up, freaking' 19-year old but still behaved like a confused cow.

The teens dozed, the movie played on, the only foreseeable danger was of the Aunts walking in. She prepared herself, looked down, his hand reflected the dim TV light.

Okay, time to find out, take it to the next level, 'ooh its cold', she murmured to nobody in particular, no one noticed, she casually pulled a sheet over her legs, pushed the waistband of her tights down, gripped his hand and thrust it between her legs, and again crossed them tight.

Phew! That was fast, she leaned back on her arms, legs steady, 'your call Chris, I can't do more than that,' she thought, and giggled at her recklessness but now she didn't care. Anything was better than NOT KNOWING she thought while drunk with elation. Stop lying witch, you already know.

Surprise of surprises, The Sphinx showed signs of life after all. His fingers moved, his touch was soothing, gentle, light, his fingers tried to slip in; and then - several things happened at once - he felt her, knew her, his hand was immobile, was he stunned? He turned to stare, probably couldn't stop himself, or did she imagine it?

'Yes Chris', she gave an imperceptible nod, mouthed silently, 'for you.'

There was a long silence, she was afraid, what if he pulled out? His fingertips moved again while she exhaled a sigh of relief. He gently stroked her swollen lips, while the tension abated, and then shifted his attention to her cherry. She couldn't hold back her tears; they streamed silently down her cheeks. She turned sideways to hide them, didn't want him to see, 'I made it, Santa Maria Mother of God, I made it.'

Suddenly she knew it was time, he continued to stroke her gently while she wanted him to, both, stop, as well as continue. This was going out of control, her mouth opened, she tried to say something but couldn't and then, she let it go.

She came like a waterfall, with a roar in her ears, saw sparklers with her eyes shut, this was freaky, what had happened, where was she, was she alive, was she in heaven? Couldn't see, just feel, 'Oh oh no', she gasped with eyes shut, blinked them open, everything was just the same as before; and Chris, where was his hand, her knees jerked up, okay, he was still in there.

Look around you Witch; everything's the same as before, no freakin' debris, no explosion, only you. She looked down, the sheets were soaked and her tights were wet. She didn't have to look down to find out; that she knew - she'd been on Route-66 before.

His hand moved again, déjà vu did they call it? Gentle strokes swelled her again. 'No oh No, No, No,' she begged with her eyes, 'I'll scream', he was cruel, stared flatly at the screen with a wry smile. Was he teasing her? If yes, she deserved it.

A call from inside, 'Angiiiiiiiieeeeeeeee.'

'Yes Auntie.' She giggled at the hypocrisy of it all, wake up Witch, don't go numb, she moved the dry part of the sheet between her legs before she came again, less violently but equally blissful. Yes, she'd visited Canada just now - this was the freakin' Niagara.

Phew, was she drained out. A second yell, wake up witch, time to move, sounds from the passage, his hand was out; did it glisten or did she imagine it?

Her thoughts were rambled; she focused on the movie, saw that it was coming to a close. The teens were fast asleep. Suddenly she sensed a movement, she'd forgotten all about him. He leaned towards her and whispered, 'Baby, possible to see you tomorrow?'

She caught a whiff of cologne, Jovan Sex Appeal, she knew it.

He continued, 'not here,' and paused, 'outside.'

What did he mean, she didn't care, shook her head 'yes' dumbly, she was tongue-tied again, like a zombie.

'Text me when you wake up', he said again, then got up abruptly and left.

Another call, 'Angie, get in right now.'

She looked down to witness the frightful freakin' mess. She was weak; her knees trembled as she got up, a kaleidoscope of emotions churned in her skull. She was sleepy, excited and satisfied all at once, she jumped up, her thoughts awhirl, like the time she was drunk for the first time.

'That reminds me, I'm thirsty', she thought and went to the kitchen, picked up a drink in the light of the refrigerator; gulped it down to steady her frayed nerves, phew . . . the cold Lemon-Crush felt good, soothed her.

She was finally in her bed, her thoughts busy with self-recrimination. Was she ready? Would 'it' happen? Or would a moral lecture ensue? I'll kill him first, no no, only herself. No, I'll first make him even if he doesn't want to (like you did today witch?), were her final thoughts as her head hit the pillow and she fell asleep.

4 - SWEET LITTLE LIES

The day dawned bright and fair; early morning sun streamed through the open window. Her head throbbed at the brightness, her ears registered the scream and yell of children at play, tiny fingers yanked her hair, woke up groggy eyed, one of the kids grinned at her, he wanted to play, she threw a pillow at him while trying her best to sleep...

'Wake up sleepy head' said one of her aunts.

Her brain finally started working - where was she last night?

LAST NITE?... OMG, she sprang out of bed, had to get dressed quick, time check - it was 10, her mum would be proud today.

She brushed her teeth and ran to the living room - empty!!! Where was everyone? She grabbed a 4-year old, 'So kids, what's the plan?'

'We're going to Oceanário.'

'Angie's coming too', one of the Aunts beamed, 'correct dear?' Though the way the witch said it, it sounded more of a fact than a query.

'Sorry Auntie, I've got classes', Oh Oh, wake-up witch

today's Saturday!!! 'Extra classes' she mumbled weakly.

The lie compounded with another screw-up: Aunt Rita was within earshot and heard; she got a hard stare. Angie blushed, looked down, no freakin' use, she couldn't hide anything from her. Aunt Rita knew her through 'n through, had taken care of her since she was born; the other cows looked suspicious but didn't protest.

Aunt Rita said dryly, 'Never mind, you can tell your mother, she's on her way.'

Phew. She was off the hook. Thank Goodness for that bit of news, she reacted as if an electric jolt had hit her. She knew she had to disappear or her story would end here and now.

'Really sorry, she mumbled, 'Aunts 'n sweethearts, I've to leave but we'll meet soon.'

She noticed Chris wasn't there, 'Where's Uncle Chris', she asked, keeping her innocent, casual and light.

'He's out for the day, had some work.'

Work did he call it? Hee hee, she knew what that meant. Or did it? She gulped down her hot-chocolate, ran to the bath, her brain processed at the speed of light.

She was finished an hour later - showered, scrubbed and ready to go. She'd left the stubble on her armpits, no time to worry about that now, she'd let it stay. What about the honey-grove? Her hair was soft, wispy and untrimmed; they say it got rough if you used a razor. Forget it, she thought, despite last night she still didn't believe 'it' would happen. Anyway, there was no time to waste; she'd to get out as fast as she could.

She checked her clothes, black tees to work some black magic, hee hee. Check panties – white cotton with a bunnies imprint. Would they do? They'd looked cute when she'd bought them, now they appeared stupid and childish. Why didn't she have those flimsy black-string ones? 'Coz they'd attract unwelcome attention, that's why. Concentrate witch, anything else?

It was time to do last minute checks - Listerine - check, comb - check, Chanel Allure – check, cell – check; money – check; gum – check; great, she was good to go; it was time to get dressed. She hopped on one leg to put on her jeans with one hand and deftly flicked her nails on her cell with the other.

Her text: 'I'm up.'

His: 'Reach Rue das Fontainhas, your time, take a cab:-)'

Stay cool, witch, nonchalant: 'Ohhhkayy :-)'

She knew the place, it'd take the better part of an hour - hurry, hurry, hurry witch, she goaded herself; today's the day of her destiny.

Her cousins sulked, she kissed them goodbye, an extra cuddle for Aunt Rita; she still wouldn't look her in the eye; said goodbye to her Aunts, suspicious glares bored into her from all around but they couldn't do a thing - except lock her up of course.

She said goodbye to the bleary eyed Porcos as well. Why was it so difficult getting out of here? Guantanamo Bay inmates had it easy she thought, as she scampered out of the Block, glad that she was athletic. She quickly flagged a cab across the road and settled herself down for the long drive ahead.

Her cell beeped, 'Angie, why aren't you coming with us to Oceanário?' her mother whined.

'Extra classes Mumma, and I don't want to get bored babysitting stupid kids.'

A quick, 'Take care, we'll miss you hon,' her mom was probably on speaker-phone! Hee hee, she did that at times.

She checked her nails – nodded approvingly. What about her hair? Probably needs the brush again; Shoes? Stupid sneakers; she wailed, where was style when she needed it. It was never this way in the movies.

Oh, shut-up witch, this is real-life. She felt impatient, restless; and closed her eyes to pray. Her choices were simple, 'Please Santa Maria, don't make my brain go numb, or let me say or do something dumb. 'And, just this once,' she gulped and added as an afterthought, 'please-please-please make 'it' happen.'

She was apprehensive, what if he lectured her, moralised her or scolded her even? The thought agonised her, she had her pride, she'd never see him again, she'd. . .

They'd arrived; he was there; she got off while he paid the cab. She couldn't look him in the eye, fumbled with her satchel while her heart hammered and brain searched for something clever to say, but 'Hi Uncle Chris' was all that she could manage.

Screw it, she thought, why should this time be any different? The restlessness left her, she threw her arms around him, like always and felt his after-shave; the warmth of weak winter sunshine on her back; he gave her a close hug and took her satchel.

'This way', he said, she tried to keep pace; he had long legs; he led the way, she skipped after him and then they were at Francesinha. He pushed open the glass door.

'I've had grub.'

'Still, a quick bite, Baby', he said with a half-smile.

She ordered a frango and coke while he had bifanas and coffee. She looked around, spied an early-afternoon crowd; tourists, teens, kids, no office-goers this early in the day.

She soaked in the atmosphere excitedly - she felt comfortable, loose, cheerful - and wanted to talk. She prattled-on, she didn't know what - something about her classes, how she got here – soon it was just like old times, when he'd take her to MacDonald's and she'd order till she burst; but that was before she was 14.

Wait! He'd said something; didn't catch; the freakin' racket in the background.

She leaned forward as his voice was almost a whisper. Her brows quizzed, 'What Chris?' she asked with her frank, open, honest, child-like eyes.

Why was he so freakin' preoccupied? OMG, last night!!! She'd forgotten why she was here; he looked down for an instant then directly into her eyes - she was terrified. Would he moralise her?

Stella Marie Mother of God if he did, it was over. She'd walk out. She didn't care. Anything was better than the humiliation she'd feel; yes, she would cry for the rest of her life but she'd never see him again. That much she knew. She'd kill herself; her mind wandered again, her thoughts trailed-off . . .

He interrupted the chain, his voice louder, firmer, 'Shall we, Sweetheart?' He picked up her satchel and started walking away.

A flash of irritation belied her tension, 'shall we WHAT you freakin moron,' as she hurried behind him, 'why wouldn't he spell it out?'

Her heart hammered against her ribs, it could mean only one thing – or could it, witch? Maybe he doesn't want to humiliate you in public; she looked down and nodded while her blood pounded in her ears.

Despite her pulse rate she felt it was time to assert herself. 'Where to, Chris?'

She'd called his name – as an equal - did he notice? He still called her Baby.

'Surprise, Baby.'

Her head spun; she was too terrified to think. Once again, what next? Would he scold her? Would he tell her mother? Or had he told her already? Would she find the entire clan waiting there, for her, to declare judgment? To make an example of her, to the younger pre-teens even? Should she get out now? Run, while she still had the chance? But where could she go?

She could never bear the shame, the sordid soap opera, it'd be horrid, worse than the punishment which she now felt she richly deserved. She'd be sent away for sure, to a Catholic nunnery; but then what about last night? Big deal, it was she who'd pushed it; she'd read too much into one stupid small incident.

No, she was right in what she'd done. Screw it, anything was better than the suspense, another few moments and she'd know.

She half-walked, half-ran behind him; her hands locked with his, their fingers entwined communicated an intimacy, an under-current, a knowledge that this was different, somehow, from other days. She struggled to keep pace. She was breathless with excitement, expectation and foreknowledge; he, impervious to her discomfort, pulled, no - almost dragged her ahead.

'Wait Chris,' she cried, 'please.'

He slowed down but not much.

5 - ZOMBIE

They'd arrived at an apartment block. He entered it and climbed quickly up the stairs to the 2nd floor and fumbled for the keys. It was the first time he'd left her hand since the café. She stood in terrified silence, didn't utter a word, it was as if she knew – knew what witch? He unlocked the door, turned, it was alright; the look in his eyes said it all, words were unnecessary.

He pulled her with one hand, she dropped her satchel to the ground, he lifted her like a toy and walked inside while she kicked her sneakers off; and then they were in the living room, their lips devoured each other frantically, her lips went wild, all over his face while her heart hammered. She was afraid it would burst.

Phew, time to come up for air. He gently pulled her head back by her hair, steadied her, his lips were on hers again, their mouths locked, and, after what seemed to her an awfully short time, he pulled out, recovered, took a deep breath and was back at it again.

He murmured, 'Strawberry . . .'

She giggled - she knew what he meant. He'd taught her to brush her tongue, till it was 'strawberry red'; she slipped it out cautiously, gasped, surprised with the violence with which he sucked, so hard, it hurt, almost pulled it out of its sockets.

'Witch, do tongues have sockets'; mmm, mmmmm, she moaned in protest, half-heartedly - she knew, it was delicious, heady, a freakin' drug. He released the pressure, though only slightly; she was still firmly lodged in his mouth.

Her poor bruised tongue was back, he nibbled her lips, she surfaced, shuddered, took a deep breath, she was too shy to meet his eyes while her thoughts raced, 'What next?' she filled with a warm feeling, was swollen; at least she knew what THAT was, thank-goodness; damp and hot.

His shirt was off; there was a strange glazed look on his face, which she saw for the first time. She thought it 'funny'; like what people who wear spectacles had when they'd take them off, and blinked. Or a zombie in the Americano horror movies, more comedy than horror she'd say . . . but she was digressing.

He pulled her towards him and took her Tee and bra off in one goes; unbuttoned her jeans and pushed them down with his feet. Her face was red, eyes shut tight with shame - her white cotton panties probably appeared childish. She wished she'd paid greater attention to Cintia, taken lessons perhaps; and then they were off. She opened her eyes to catch his stare, felt shy, looked down, at her small unripe mangoes, and her raisins were erect – they embarrassed her. Her face burnt with shame, was he disappointed?

He noticed, 'What?'

'Wish I was fair,' she lied while thinking of something clever to say.

'No way', he smiled, 'dark skin attracts like a magnet does.'

'And red?'

'An attribute of nobility and an instant turn-on,' he grinned.

His hands explored her, they were light and warm on her shoulders, steady, loving, possessive (wake up witch) his eyes were still busy, drinking her in.

'Your skin is actually red', he said in a matter-of-fact voice, 'I thought it was only your hair.'

'Do you like what you see Chris?' Her throat choked, what a stupid inane thing to say. Not her fault though, what kind of conversation was possible between a fully dressed adult and a stripped teen?

'This is heaven Baby', he pulled her to him.

Phew, it was a relief not to meet his eyes. His hands were busy in a different way, she thought, more professional (Shut up you dumb stupid witch) as they moved over the crevices, clefts and valleys of her body. They moved further down, explored her dampness, reached up, cupped her mangoes, squeezed, pinched, she yelped when he bit her raspberries, kissed her on her neck, nibbled her ears, lips and tongue; his hands were electric, she couldn't look in his eyes, but couldn't concentrate either.

Look for something to do instead. She peeked over his shoulder, there was a painting, tall-masts, warships, probably commemorating the Anglo-Portuguese Treaty of 1373, the oldest alliance still in-force in the world; this was a tasteful, nicely decorated flat, it belonged to a man though; her mind rambled on, his hands were busy stroking her all over the place, she was in teen-heaven.

He'd paused. He looked at her as if something was expected, but what? Her quizzical look betrayed her innocence; his hands on her shoulders; a gentle push down; she knelt, confused, glanced behind, the bed was visible, inside, then what were they doing here, his hand behind her head, her nose pushed against him, bumped against the shape in his jeans; she understood.

He unbuttoned them, kicked them aside; she pulled down the waistband of his shorts and opened her eyes wide at first sight, her turn to stare.

'What?' he asked

'It's beautiful', she said. She thought she knew what to do, had heard about it, talked about it, seen it dozens of times on www.xnxx.com, it was favourite with her crowd, especially during all-girl nite-outs, when they'd link their laptops to a large TV screen.

She hesitated, then with a 'Oh what the Hell!!!' thought, grabbed the shaft, opened her mouth; paused; too big, enormous, couldn't take it in, disappointed, 'It's not going to happen', she thought, 'this can never go in me', thought of what Cintia would say, her friends would laugh, felt the heat of embarrassment, it burnt her, made her cheeks redder.

His hands fondled her hair, pulled her head back, nudged her face between his legs, rubbed his shaft on her nose, mouth, forehead, pushed her face to bury it between, she tried to move, he didn't let her, tightened his grip instead, she relaxed, let him do what he wants, her mind rambled on.

She'd done the impossible, made it so far, wasn't easy, she had this fantasy for so long, her cheeks were wet, tears signified a release of pent-up emotion, she was grateful she wasn't visible, it'd been a close-run thing, what if she'd missed? She trembled at the thought, recalled Cintia bleating's, 'try it with someone your age first, it's easier', that was unthinkable, but she knew what she'd meant; i.e. NOW, smaller therefore easier, oh well, might as well go through with it.

Was she relieved it wouldn't happen? Didn't know, her

feelings were mixed, if not now – then when, maybe when she was older, but how much older??? Did she mean bigger? Didn't know, she'd apologise, make a promise, to keep herself as she was now for later.

'Poor Chris', she thought, 'it's not his fault, I'm a tease, I led him to it.' She felt sorry for him, for leading him on; if the last few moments were an indicator, she knew that he'd be disappointed, for sure!!!

His hands stopped pushing, held her firmly by the hair, guided himself, she understood, the shaft was pointing at her, she could take it in only partially, he appeared to wait, was something expected? Her call, but what?

He understood, took her hand, wrapped it around him, wake up stupid Witch, yes, recall the mpeg-clips, she gripped the thick shaft, moved her thin wrist.

'Owww ooow ooow, that hurt', he cried, what was wrong, dumb Witch, why didn't she take lessons from Cintia, why didn't she prepare herself, she repeated.

He'd said something, too busy to catch, where did you screw up, it was difficult to look up; she raised her eyebrows, quizzically, strained to listen.

'It's softer than your eyelids,' he mumbled, 'wet it Baby.'

How? Did he mean spit? Must be, she pulled back, worked up her mouth, drooled down the shaft and moved her hands again, it was smoother, gentler, faster, easier, 'so that's why', she thought; her hands had done magic, he grew bigger, if that was possible, her wrists slid faster-and-faster, just when she thought she'd 'got it' his hands tugged at her shoulders, impatient, 'there's more to be done', she wanted to tell him, but he pulled out, lifted her and walked to the bed in one smooth fluid motion.

'What a let-down', her mind ten steps ahead, 'I'm a tease', she thought again, 'I really am, hope he forgives me';

she was serious about lessons, from Cintia, or anyone else for that matter, but that was later; for the moment, things were happening too fast.

He placed her on the bed gently, adjusted her head on the pillow, turned, came back with two thick towels, placed them under her butt, 'What for', she quizzed with her eyes, he smiled, oh yes, he remembers last nite, when she wet the sheets, but it was dark then, how did he know, puzzled, didn't matter, let it go.

6 - SACRED GROVE

She closed her eyes, 'If we're not going to make love, let him do what he wants', she savoured the moment, 'I'll make up for it', she thought, 'but how?'

He was back, kissed her, neck, ears, down to her raisins, they were erect, took them in his mouth, one at a time, bit gently, she jumped, it was an electric jolt, her body was aflame, 'suck them,' she whispered hoarsely, immediately ashamed, what was happening to her?

He did, she loved it, jumped once more, they were tender; he bit them gently while gently squeezing the other with one hand. She moaned when he moved to her armpits to lick them.

She was hot, feverish, tickled, 'sorry, I haven't,' she paused, apologetically, ' . . hair,' her voice shrunk to an embarrassed whisper.

'I like it better this way, Baby', he said and continued on the other one.

'Would he - Wouldn't he? 'Go down, she thought, as according to Cintia, Catholic Men disdained from that kind of stuff, it was unmanly. But she'd seen it on www.xnxx.com, but who knew if what it showed was true.

That was an Americano site after all. She wanted him to, was she required to say something to that effect? Or lie down quietly like a pliant newly married bride as her mother kept hammering into her brain she must do as and when she got married... Whom to? She wondered...

She jerked back to consciousness. Her question had been answered. Her legs went immobile as he moved down to her bellybutton, nibbling, down- down–down then stopped to stare, she froze, 'What're you looking at?'

'At your honey-grove', he smiled.

She asked, 'Do I have one?' innocence outlined in her eyes.

He smiled, his eyes were 'funny'; some part of her brain began to comprehend, the look reminded her of a Zombie, she thought. Now what? He was really going down all the way to, - like her friends called it, the Honey-Grove.

This was terrific. Wow, www.xnxx.comwas true then, men actually did it; not just act. She knew was hot and swollen with anticipation. The thought of his mouth 'down there' electrified her already taut nerves stretched to the limit. Her head buzzed, naked electricity, wake up Witch, keep your eyes wide open, don't miss the first time – But, oh no, she suddenly realised something was wrong!!!.

He raised her knees, gently prised her open, stroked her, played with her, she was red, shamefaced, he heard her sob, she pulled her knees close.

He was puzzled, 'What Baby?'

'I haven't... y'know..', too shy to say it, she mumbled, 'hair..'

He lifted her chin, waited till she opened her eyes, face serious; smiled 'never do that Baby - I like candy floss', and waited for her to acknowledge.

She nodded, legs wide open, he was busy again, she was curious; peeked shyly - he was playing with her cherry now, 'what are these for, Chris?'

'Leaves, for protection', and bent down.

She bucked! Like a freakin' electric shock!!! This was way-way-way different from his fingers; I can't take it, she thought.

'Ooow, you almost broke my nose', he said, went down again.

She jumped once more pushed her pelvic to one side, 'sorry Chris.'

He smiled, understood, she was hypersensitive, he grasped her ankles tight, before going down for the third time, she instinctively tried to lift herself, no use, he held her down at the honey-grove, neck and shoulder muscles taut, pressed hard, his hands locked her legs, before taking her in once more, she jerked, spasmodic, her brain had shut, her body was a mass of sensation, oh no, she thought, she couldn't hold back any longer, she came in his mouth, he drank her, greedily, it seemed, he was about to pull out, 'no Chris, this is cruel', she wanted to scream, 'please don't stop', she was soaked, wanted more.

'Can you close your eyes Baby', his voice was soft, soothing, 'for just half a minute?'

How you freakin' moron, she wanted to scream, held herself back, what was happening to her? Was this her? Was this what she'd dreamt about? Her behavior was terrible; she was ashamed at once, agreed to what he'd said.

He pulled his mouth back, sat up, she was on the razor's edge of desire; screw him; she opened her eyes, saw him tear something from a small paper jacket, put it on, between his legs, she remembered, had seen Cintia show it to her once, was dazed, 'what for', she wanted to ask.

7 - SUPERNOVA

He was on top of her with one arm, a sudden move, caught her unawares, his mouth covered hers, she could feel a sweet after-taste, the scent was familiar, she puzzled over it, it wasn't coffee, and she'd not seen him drink anything; then it hit her, OMG, it was her! Was this what she tasted like? The sensation was definitely creepy, but pleasant from his perspective!!! Shut up Witch, how do you know his perspective, did he tell you? Anyway, a lot more was happening down there.

His fingers had prised her open, to nudge something firmly in place, she was confused, mumbled, 'No Chris, it's too big, won't go in', but didn't he know that already? Her hands were pushing him down, 'want you back down there', she whispered.

He smiled, that strange zombie look, his mouth covered hers completely now, gripped her thin wrists in one hand, 'What's this?' she thought; and found out the hard way.

WHAM!!!No other word better explained it!!!He ripped into her, tore her to shreds, 'Noooooooooooo', she screamed, or tried to, couldn't, her mouth was locked, struggled, he held her down, his chest crushed her in place, her legs flailed wildly, met thin air.

She was surrounded in a sea of pain, pain and more pain,

everything looked red, he was inside, pushed further, stop there's no space, her senses screamed, stop-stop-stop-stop-stop-stop No-No-No I can't, please-please-please Chris don't do this to me, No-No-No-No-No-No. . .

He was deaf, the pain rocked her pelvis, shot-up her spine, shook her, lifted the top of her skull off, she shuddered, arched, lifted him for a fraction of a second; and then he was in, she felt wet, not cum, something else.

She was filled, did he feel sorry for her, 'coz he was pulling out, phew; she was relieved, though still surrounded by a sea of pain. He was back, no pause this time, didn't let go, pounded, he was unstoppable, the rhythm increased, her head slammed against the bed-rest rest in sync, the thrusts became wilder, the pain worsened, she was incoherent, racked her brain, her body, increased in intensity.

'Stop it, please stop, 'she cried, forcing her legs wider, not possible, they were stretched to the limit, trying to withstand the exceptionally violent assault on the body and soul . She stared at the fan, the ceiling, lift-off, the top of her skull was blown away, she saw stars and stripes - red, white and blue, and then a blinding flash of light, it was over, she couldn't feel a thing, she was in outer space.

Muted strains of traffic, raindrops on her face, was it a dream, where was she, she'd never woken up like this before, strange unreal, was she outside, then recollected, gasped, opened her eyes.

Chris on the bedside, sprinkling droplets of water on her, 'My precious Baby', he whispered, 'am so sorry for hurting you', his expression more articulate than his words; she gave a weak smile, or tried her best to.

Was it over, she looked down, couldn't see, felt herself gingerly, she was swollen, tender to the touch, she felt twice, no thrice her normal size, a dull ache replaced the sharp pain.

She whispered, 'How long?' She was woolly headed; her feelings resembled a state when she and Cintia got drunk.

'Almost an hour, Baby, I let you sleep', he had a couple of white tablets in his palm, 'here, swallow these.'

'What for?' she quizzed.

'Pain-killers', he said.

'No Chris', she replied.

He was surprised, 'Why Baby?'

'I want the pain, to remind myself of you; my first time.'

He kissed her lightly on the lips, 'I'm so sorry Baby', he was contrite, 'you're very tender,' he smiled, 'but strong. You were terrific Baby, thank you.'

'Don't thank me Chris', weak smile, 'I wanted you too . . .' her voice trailed off.

She wanted to continue, to speak her heart out, 'I wanted you so bad, it hurt a million times more than it could possibly do now', but kept silent. . . smiled, she'd done 'it.'

She wanted to pee, tried to get up, pushed her legs off the bed, wanted to stand, the room swam; she'd have fallen, her legs were rubber, he caught her.

'Blood loss, Baby, have some of this', he had a chilled glass of Lemon Crush in his hand, something reddish floated in swirls.

'I'll throw-up.'

He reassured her, 'No, you won't.'

She gulped it down, Lemon Crush and Tabasco . . . mmmmmm, the right stuff, where do they teach this.

'Time?' She quizzed.

'Almost 12, hungry?'

'Nooooooooo', she mock-drawled, 'wanna be with you.'

They kissed, he was soft and gentle, 'Walk slow, keep

your balance', he said.

She waited, legs down gingerly, not so bad, just like when she had the curse, but the reasons here were different.

He supported her, walked her to the bath, she went in and closed the door.

Look down, do a quick inventory check - flecks of dried blood between her legs, she felt exposed, raw, bruised, wait, look around; she saw something in the corner, white towels, reddish in the centre, weird design, curious, picked it up, 'OMG', so much blood, it was hers, had to be, she dropped it, took another, cleaned up.

Opened the cabinet, well-equipped, spare toothbrushes, after-shave lotion, soap, someone had done their homework, but this was not a woman's bath; she pulled out a toothbrush, looked in the mirror, almost screamed with fright - Who was this Witch? Had to be her!!! What a freakin' train-wreck!!! Fit for Halloween night!!! Her hair was all over the place, lipstick streaks on her cheeks, no guesses for what you've been upto Witch, thank Santa Maria this didn't happen at home, Cintia was right after all.

But wait, what was different? Something certainly was, but what? It was her, how, why? Shook her head to think clearly, couldn't place it; did a double take on the mirror; her lip had a slight curl, sardonic perhaps; or was it in her eyes; or her imagination? Maybe, she was unsure, but yes, the look was familiar, somewhat condescending, like what Cintia always had, while she described what 'it' felt like.

Soft knock on the door, his whisper, 'Angie.'

Something's wrong, he'd never called her Angie before . . . unless he was really stressed out.

She hesitated, not for that, but because she didn't want to be seen this way - not a stitch on. She groped for something to cover-up . . . nothing.

He read her mind, 'Don't bother Baby. Let me in.'

Quick look in the mirror, screw it, there was no time for make-up. She turned and opened the latch.

8 - IN THRU' THE OUT DOOR

He rushed in, impatient and eager, pulled her into his arms and continued to kiss her; his hands were cupped over her butt. She felt him on her stomach, he was a rock, but she wasn't ready.

'Not now', she begged, 'please Chris, I'm not in the mood.'

'It has to be done', he sounded strange; his voice was thick, strangled? Something weird about his behavior made her glance sharply at him – she saw the look on his face – Was it guilt? Or Fear? Of what? That she'd refuse? But what? Or was it desire? Or all at once? Anyway, there was no time to think - things were moving too fast.

She also knew that look in his eyes – which said it all. The look her instinct told her she'd grow to recognise. It was 'The Zombie' and it meant 'it's pointless to reason.'

Funny, he'd turned her around, hugged her tight, she felt his heat, kill me, here and now she thought, what better way to die?

His hand was on the shower knob, 'Wet your hair?' he asked.

'Uh huh….' she mumbled, did it matter, if one was

dead? Like live bait on a hook is what she felt like.

He turned the shower on, gelled her expertly with liquid soap, 'ready Baby?'

Realisation dawned. Oh no-o-o-o-o, he wanted her by the fudge chute for Crissakes! One last try to get away, 'Why Chris, why here,' she blurted, 'why now?' though she knew, how she couldn't say – that he wouldn't listen.

He pushed her feet apart; his arm firmly encircled her waist.

She supported herself, her chest against the shower taps, rested her head on the wall; somehow this had gone horribly wrong. She just wanted to die – finish it all.

His voice interrupted her chain of thoughts, 'Ready Baby?'

She gasped, 'mm mm', just wanted it to be over.

He was in. This was freakin' agony, a different kind of pain, he moved, freakin' hell, wrenching, dull, heavy, throbbing pain, he'd hit a nerve, somewhere deep in her which blazed a path all the way to the pin-receptors in her brain.

'It hurts,' she whimpered, unable to breathe, 'so much.'

'You're too tight', he mumbled, she could make out that he was hoarse with desire. He moved slowly, gently at first, 'loosen up, Baby,' was the last thing he said before pushing forcefully all the way in.

She tried, it was no freakin' use, why was he talking Greek?

'Let me bear it for him, please', her thighs took the punishment, her elfin body shuddered with pain, she almost slipped but held her ground, 'please don't let me fall', she thought.

The pain increased, no use, he was on his own weird trip, his pace increased, hammered her, head slammed against the wall, the bones of her chest bruised against the shower taps.

She could only pray, 'Santa Maria, Mother of God, Help me, Help me, Help me'; Like asking for a freakin' miracle!!! But something did happen, her back had arched – on its own or was it her? Or was it a reflex action? Wish she knew, but this was it, she felt better instantly, how easy, when compared to before, the pain had reduced, she arched her back to the maximum, phew – she breathed out, this was much-much-much better, too tight, but still better. She was relieved that she could bear it now, and who knows, she may grow to like it even? But that was later, not now, this was a violation of the senses, of her freedom, of her . . . couldn't concentrate, screw it!!! She mocked herself, Yeah, Baby that's right!!!

Racks of pain beat her, in rhythm, punished her frail body, she whimpered in sync, keep standing, don't fall, she wouldn't, this much she knew, think something else; look aside, through the window, houses opposite, curtains fluttered in the breeze, this was an area for singles, modest, economical, well connected, surrounded with places to eat, wham, slam, bang, the pace increased, knew it was time, felt him tense, 'time to wake up Witch', she admonished herself, almost there, concentrate, keep your balance, till . . . he exploded. Molten metal shot inside her in a constant stream. He kept at it for a long time – even after he'd cum (was that what they called it?), filled her, till he was spent.

He held her tight, his heart slammed against her back, his breath rushed in her ears, 'sorry Baby, couldn't help it', he panted, breathless, 'Wanted it so bad, waited forever.'

She was pleased, though taken aback by his frank admission. What was that again? She was, surprised, at a loss for words, embarrassed even.

And then, 'God, you're strong.'

She was grateful for 'that', I'm not a loser after all, she

thought. But she had to make him know how she felt - 'That's okay Chris', she said, her voice weak — but strong as steel, 'but now can I have time to myself now?'

He wouldn't meet her gaze, he looked down, nodded and went out.

9 - ANACONDA

Ages later, she was out, presentable, damp, towel wrapped around her; Chris stared at her, she blushed, looked down, still couldn't meet his eyes, he pushed her on the bed, took her in his arms, cuddled her like a Baby.

She loved it, though still sore, bruised, in pain but felt warm and wonderful.

She noticed a tray on the bed, sandwiches, Lemon Crush, cheese, an omelette, she nibbled, she wasn't in a mood to eat; he forced her, it was pointless to resist.

She felt drowsy, sleepy; wiped her mouth with a tissue; sipped Lemon Crush - mmmmm, felt nice; it was laced with Tabasco, would it be their trademark for this?

'No time to sleep now, Baby', he said, 'we've to be out by 4', he bent down, munched her raisins like chewing gum; the little scamps had a will of their own, were erect in an instant.

He sat up, 'Uh. . . '

She sensed it, 'What Chris? 'He didn't reply.

'Say it.'

He didn't meet her eyes, 'Can I squeeze?'

'Phew!' She giggled with relief, 'Sure Chris, anything you

want.'

'It will hurt.'

Compared to the past hour? That was a laugh!!! She was nonchalant, 'mmm hmmm', why were Men so freakin' dumb, not their fault, it was their genetic make-up, 'Relax Chris; just do what you want to,' she wanted to add, 'I'm yours after all,' but she'd leave that for later.

He started, with both palms, it became rougher, he squeezed tighter, she winced, did he notice? No, the Zombie was back, was crushing her puppies.

Wait!!! She discerned the current, a vibration, which she'd grown to recognise - he wanted something else, was again too embarrassed to tell.

She encouraged him, 'What Chris?'

'Can I bite?' he asked, 'won't break skin.'

'Sure Chris', no sooner had he started that she regretted it, 'Ouch.'

'Mmmmm, sorry Baby', he was busy, she liked him this way, on her chest, didn't know why, her raisins were bruised and quickly swelled to twice their size; he was engrossed, busy at it, her thoughts rambled.

Her mind recollected visions of a school visit to a Farm - the cows, the stables, a performance by the cowboys, a spectacular display, of a horse being broken in, an enraptured audience, during question time she'd queried, 'Why do you call it breaking-in?'

'It's not natural', they explained, 'no horse likes to carry a weight for life, but then it does when we're through.'

'Breaking-in' was apt for her too; she was broken, ripped, split, front, back, sucked, squeezed, bitten - was anything else left? She sighed, looked down, he munched her raspberries in peaceful bliss, she felt the dampness creep back; her body, though bruised, also had a will of its own.

What about him? She felt him stir - No Way was she going through that again! She may look dumb but she wasn't stupid, she wouldn't let him take her now.

But what if the Zombie comes back? She had to make her move. She pushed him away with a coy smile and said, 'Can't let you do all the work, Chris, my turn now', and moved down.

He was pleasantly surprised, smiled; nodded his acceptance; men were naturally dumb, he hadn't realised what had just happened.

She closed her fist over him; felt something soft, non-threatening; 'what's this?' she quizzed, eyebrows raised curiously.

'The snake, Baby, check out the parts.'

Her eyes widened to get a better look; she felt his hand behind her head.

He said, 'Should I explain?'

'Uh huh.'

He pointed out, 'This is the hood, here's the drawstring, the shaft, the vein, the nuts and root.'

She was a quick learner, grasped it all, and examined him carefully, probed with thin precise fingers; asked 'What's the vein?'

'It's squeezed to retain the blood for a few extra moments, as well as to empty it after . . .' his voice trailed off.

'And the root?'

'The Root of All Evil', he smirked, 'Baby, that's where all the nerves are; and where you work when you play Snake Charmer', he explained with a smile, 'and on a side-note, always wet it 'coz it hurts.'

Great, she got it in an instant; she was reminded of Dors

VENABILI, Hari SELDON's human-looking robot.

Time to start, yeah, she was a freakin' robot, time to work up drool, spit, grip the shaft, wet the head, take it in, work the tongue and the wrists; it was smaller and, therefore, easier; She felt in control.

He grew. She flicked her fingers faster and looked up with an impish smile.

He leaned back, 'You're terrific Baby,'

She felt him tense up, recalled the lesson, and closed the vein tight.

'No, Baby, please' he moaned, 'when did you learn to do that?'

'Just now.'

'You're terrific Baby, too smart for any man.'

'Not terrific', she mumbled, couldn't talk with mouth full, 'I'm an accountant.'

The moment closed in, she felt him tense up, she let go the pressure, caught the jet-stream at the back of her throat; kept up the pace, received the aftershocks till he was limp.

She still worked ceaselessly, her tongue and fingers busy, probed, pushed, to bring the dead tissue to life, worked her wrists furiously to squeeze him out, counted 1, 2, 3 to 10 till it was dry and limp.

She let him stay in her mouth, glanced up, he was soaked with perspiration and couldn't talk, his eyes looked drugged, he saw her, struggled to speak, she felt the reversal of roles, she was in control, yet there were hints of still life.

You're strong as well Uncle Chris, she thought.

'Keep your head back', she said and continued to play the root with her fingers; moments later, he was up, weak but up; she kept at it unsparingly, wouldn't let go.

'No, please no, Baby, I'll die' he protested.

'No way, Chris, you're mine now', she felt her power, so this was it felt to have someone at your mercy, this was The 'Original' Secret, so long Rhonda BRYNE, a weak push upwards, a final spasm, and then it was over - victory, she'd done it!!!

'Phew, that was hard work', she giggled.

Wait, what was this, her antennae worked overtime, she sensed something, someone was here - Who? A Presence? You're going crazy witch, shut up!!!

She let go, slipped him out, wet, limp, empty spent, yes, something was definitely happening, she looked up.

He'd opened his eyes.

And then he saw Her.

.

10 - SHEKINAH

Their eyes met; these were not the eyes of a child; a shiver crept up his spine, Her gaze scorched him.

He looked down, eyes squeezed tight, keep the tears in check; pray, quick, before she goes away.

'Santa Maria, Mãe de Deus, a minha mãe, como o

senhor, o Messias em seus braços tão perto do seu coração, segure-me agora e ouvir os gritos do meu coração. Conforto-me com o seu abraço quente. Ensina-me perfeita fé e esperança, e levar-me para o seu Filho, Jesus Cristo, meu Senhor e Salvador .'

Angie was puzzled; he looked deflated; had she seen this before? When? Where? It's important her brain said but she couldn't remember, tried to link, connect-up; to what was going on. What did it mean? Why did he act so weird? Was he crying???Yes, tears streamed fast down his sharp cheekbones.

Was she responsible? She felt it . . . somehow; but what had she done?

He was mumbling something, couldn't grasp, she strained to listen, what had he said? She shrugged, asked 'did you say something Chris?' her tone had changed, softened.

He could only nod, he knew who She was, she didn't; his throat was swollen, too choked speak.

She was worried, crawled over, held his head close to her chest; he jerked to consciousness, like someone who'd had an electric shock, she thought.

'I'll always be there for you, Chris, you know that', now what made her say that?

In any event, it was the wrong thing to say, the silent tears transformed into nerve-wracking sobs, like the release of a dam, he didn't hold them back, nor attempt to; they turned to a flood, his back and chest convulsed, couldn't catch what he'd said.

These didn't appear to be tears of anguish . . . or pain, more like release, to heal, but what? Something had happened, she mustn't pry, first let him calm down - she could check with Cintia later - do all men crack-up after a good workout? Witch, what'd 'you mean Good???

'Let it go, Chris', her fingertips gently soothed his forehead, it was hot, feverish, 'let it go.'

'Forgive me.'

'Wha..a...a...at?'

'Forgive me', he begged, 'Forgive me.'

'Okay'...weird!

'Please,' he begged, 'Say it!'

No time to argue, just say it, 'I forgive you Chris.'

His eyes closed with a smile, tears trickled down his cheeks, he was still; she checked, mystified - he'd zonked out.

11 - THE LONG GOODBYE

Eyes closed, dreamland, sounds of cutlery, she was awake, a flask, glasses, her clothes were folded neatly on the bed.

'Time?'

He showed 4 fingers.

'You have to eat, but first clean-up.'

'Why the stress on hygiene Chris?' she was curious, 'why brush so much? Your teeth will wear off.'

He smiled, 'Don't want a Michael DOUGLAS Baby, for either of us.'

She understood.

They were back in the shower, tongues probed, lips locked, bodies pressed tight, disheveled, wet.

She asked softly, 'what happened back there, Chris?'

He averted his eyes, embarrassed, mumbled, 'Tell you someday, not now.'

Don't push it; let him have his pride.

He'd made Hot Chocolate, her favourite.

'Thanx Chris.'

'Gulp it down Baby.'

She did. Then, 'I can't walk Chris.'

'It's okay Baby, I'll drop you home.'

She got up, picked up her clothes, got dressed slowly; the thought of separation was bitter, sharp, she held back tears.

He sensed it, pulled her to his chest, stroked her hair, whispered, 'Baby, Baby, rest tomorrow.'

'And then?' she cried.

'Back to work.'

She smiled, liked that, 'to work', it'd be their code.

One last kiss, nice and long and slow, and then they were on their way; she was pensive, leaned against him.

'Still hurting?'

'Uh huh, but please don't apologise!!!' She smiled, 'and Chris?'

'What Baby?'

'Why do they call it Making Love?' she asked hesitant, shy, 'it's anything but that.'

He smiled, 'You'll find out Baby', he stroked her hair.

Freakin' weird!!!

She stopped the cab some distance away.

'Sure you can make it?' he was concerned.

She didn't want him to be seen by that Witch Sequeira; always in the balcony, was sure to tell her mother.

'I'll make it', she smiled weakly.

'I'll wait till I get your text.'

She started to cry.

He held her by the shoulders, his voice ever so gentle, 'Baby, do you remember?'

She knew.

He asked, 'What?'

'No Cry No Turn back,' she lisped in a little girl voice; he'd taught her the jingle, ages ago, when she was small; 'oh well', she smiled weakly, 'I shan't then', and turned to walk away.

She took out her spare key, opened the door; checked her cell, 13 missed calls from her mother, calls from Cintia, some friends, some losers, but first Chris.

Her text, 'I'm home . . . :/'

His reply, 'Great Sweetheart, sleep tight, I'll leave now.'

Next was to her parents, 'I'm home.'

Her Dad would be there soon; she was bruised, sore, limped; the danger was her Mother, she'd guess, think fast Witch; she had to be alone tonite, call Cintia.

'Cin, can you come over?'

'Sure honey, anything special?'

Cintia, sweet as always, never asked why, always said yes.

'Mmm, yes', she modulated her voice, this had to dramatic yet cool, something like 'First step for mankind' or something similar, yeah, she knew what; first adopt a matter-of-fact tone : 'I've crossed the river.'

Cintia screamed, 'No, No, No . . . OMG, great!!! I'll be there ASAP.'

'Remember, we were together today.'

'I will, sure, she knew her mother would check.

Dinner over, after ages, her mother didn't prattled on with Cintia, she liked her; she was too busy with her thoughts and the dull sharp bursts of pain.

'What happened to your ankle?'

'Oh Aunty, Angie slipped down the stairs, but I caught her before she fell,' Cintia said.

Her mother smiled, 'You two must be rushing about as usual.'

Some TV, hot chocolate, Cintia wished them goodnite and then they were finally alone.

'Quick, tell me about it and don't hold back or I'll kill you', Cintia threatened.

'Oh, there's nothing to tell', she giggled.

Cintia was on her in a flash, slammed her head with a pillow 'You Witch', screams, yells, they were back to the

Her mother heard, 'Angiiiiiiiiiieeeeeeeeeeeeee . . .'

She could hear her mother, giggled, 'sorry Mumma', she yelled back.

'What's that witch?'

Her Tee was down to one side, Cintia pulled it down further.

'That's not all', she pulled up her Tee to reveal her raisins; bitten, swollen and blue.

'It hurts to wear a bra . . .'

Cintia gasped, 'This is crazy, why did you . . .?'

'Check this out', she pulled out her tongue, the black and blue bruise marks were prominently visible - like a combat trophy or scars after a battle.

'There's more,' she raised her sweatshirt, pulled her sleeves to give Cintia a quick glimpse of the red marks where he'd held her wrists tight. Cintia was stunned, realised what she meant.

'OMG, what an animal', she said, 'are you sure he's not a Latter Day Saint?'

'No silly, he's not' she was happy, very happy, 'it was just wild.'

'But this is criminal Angie.'

'Aw, forget it', she said, 'this is the Iberian Peninsula; to get banged about a bit in bed is as commonplace as sightings of the Holy Mother.' She continued, 'Don't you remember the case in S☐tre?'

'What about it?'

'Apparently a wife complained to the Judge for Women's Issues; about her husband literally giving it to her in bed.'

'And?'

'The judge wished it'd happen to her; and threw her out!'

They split into peals of laughter.

Cintia asked, 'When do you see him next?'

'There's a family get-together tomorrow but he's at Algarve for a week.'

'That's good, 'coz you're not going anywhere.'

They talked on through the nite; she was excited, exhausted, overcome and tired out and finally slept a couple of hours after midnite.

Prayers before a picnic; she knelt at the church of Santa Maria de Belém, begged her forgiveness, she hoped the Holy Mother would understand; Cintia tugged her, she looked up; observe silence for the hymn, accept the hostia, get blessed and they were out.

'Hypocrites, aren't we?' Cintia said.

'Don't be silly; what can you hide from the Holy Mother?'

The kids got busy, kicking, shoving, punching, gauging each other's eyes out; they sat in the back of the car; the picnic was perfunctory, wistful thoughts of Chris, she wanted to be with him, a kaleidoscope of images of yesterday juggled inside her head, she giggled.

'What?' Cintia, whispered, suspicious.

'mmm . . . nothing.'

'Him?'

'Yep.'

'Will you be there in class tomorrow?'

'I will, need to get out, need to trade notes with a professional.'

Cintia puzzled, 'Who?'

'You', impish smile.

'Shut up Witch', Cintia punched her, both of them collapsed with laughter.

II - RIDING THE SNAKE

1 - LA FLAQUEZA DEL BOLCHEVIQUE

She was chewing her pencil, dreaming of Chris when she was interrupted by the buzz of her cell.

It was his text, days later, in the middle of finance class - 'Free tomorrow?'

Her heart hammered, her mouth was dry. 'Yes :P'

Cintia noticed as well, frowned.

'How r u?'

Brain into hyper-drive, why ask AFTER if she was free? Could mean only one thing – or could it?

'Better', she lied; she was sore, still blue. Cintia took one look at her, caught on instantly, and was furious.

'Shall we, Baby?'

'Ohhhhkayyy ^_^', she tried to sound nonchalant, as if she did it everyday.

'SLUT', Cintia scribbled on her page.

'Same place, same time?'

'Earlier', she said, why lose out, she thought with a grin.

'Can't wait :)'

'Likewise.'

'Enough! Stop it. This is not happening,' Cintia scribbled on her notes.

She replied, 'He leaves on Sunday, please Cin, I beg of you.'

Cintia, annoyed, wrote again sarcastically, 'Oh I'm sorry - is it him or is it you?'

'I don't know Cintia, please, stay with me.'

'Promise me it won't be like the last time,' she wrote.

'I promise, swear, on Santa Maria.'

'Yeah, we'll see,' Cintia scribbled.

Classes were skipped for the rest of the day, they ran to prepare; Estee Lauder make-up, Nina Ricci Fantasy, Listerine strips, Lip-gloss, lingerie; anything which could be hidden under Tees, jeans and sneakers.

They stopped for a soda, giggling conspiratorially all the time; she caught Cintia staring at her.

'What?'

She said slowly, 'Did you know, your zits have disappeared.'

'Uh huh,' she was pleased, 'so there are some advantages after all.'

'I envy you', Cintia said.

'C'mon Cintia, you know all about it.'

'I know', she let out a sigh, 'I just don't know how long it'll last.'

'Oh screw it', she said, 'It's not La Flaqueza del Bolchevique.'

'How do you know?'

She giggled, 'I'm not dead yet.'

Cintia, arched her eyebrows, gave a resigned shrug, muttered dryly, 'Here we go again.'

Friday.

She took extra care to dress, did a double inventory check; her bruises had faded but were still blue; alibis had been fixed.

She recalled her text the nite before - 'Earlier Chris, more time with u.'

'Then take a cab Sweetheart.'

'^_^okiez :-)'

She put on her flimsiest underwear, pure lace, a genuine turn-on; tees and jeans had to be it; or else her romantic interlude would be nipped in the bud. Finally managed to reach the breakfast table; too excited to eat, careful, mustn't arouse suspicion, her pulse raced.

Despite the subterfuge, her mother noticed, 'you look different today, Angie.'

'Uh huh, like what Mumma?'

'You're glowing, you know that?'

She grinned, 'Thanx Mumma', that she knew why.

'I'm glad you weren't all over Chris this time.'

The thought of what had gone on was too amusing, she giggled, tried to simulate a cough, choked on her cornflakes.

'Careful Angie', her mother, all concern, 'it'll go into your windpipe.'

'Mmm huh', she could breathe again.

Her mother, warmed to the theme, continued in the same vein, 'You must spend time with boys your own age.'

'Oh Mumma', her cheeks were aflame; 'you're embarrassing me.'

It was time to disappear, she quickly gulped down her hot-chocolate, swallowed her toast with only one aim in her mind - To get out of here; fast.

'My little girl,' her mother beamed, 'see how innocently she blushes.'

She thought, 'if you only knew, witch' and raced out.

Where were the freaking cabs?

Here was one, 'On my way', she texted.

'Waitin' for u.'

Went through the drill again; her hair was brushed, skin scrubbed, she was excited, now why, witch? More of the same? No, it'd be different again. Yeah, why may I ask? She had an intuition, couldn't say why, but she knew, deep within; yeah witch, deep within your sweet-box. Awww, shut the F-up!!!

Slip a Listerine strip in her mouth, spray some more Nina Ricci 'Elixir'; what freakin' subterfuge, why didn't the world leave lovers alone. Thoughts ricocheted inside her skull; Cintia was pissed; big deal! Was she jealous? Had to be, it's different from doing it in the backseat of a car with a pimply faced idiot, bad breath and body odour; was she being unkind? Certainly, but true, the louts weren't in the same class as Chris.

C'mon, faster, you freakin' moron.

The driver was confused, 'perdão?'

'Nothing', stop it witch, don't kick the backseat.

She tried to contain her thoughts, switch to parallel processing; women's minds could think of several things at once; she knew she'd missed something yesterday, it was a 'tell', went through the events again, hot flushes on her cheeks, concentrate witch, yeah there it was - in the shower, he'd used the term 'waited forever.'

No, she hadn't missed it, was puzzled, what could it mean? To be absolutely impartial, she narrowed it down to three possibilities:-

First, he was Gay. Strike that out, she knew the answer to that.

Second, he lived in a jungle - No, Brasilia had the best lookers that side of the equator; just as she was 'The One' this side, but don't digress, witch.

Finally, he hadn't done it for a long-long-long time.

That seemed more likely, was plausible. She had proof -

the way he mauled her, for instance, went through her as if she wasn't even there. Plus, she'd noted his desperation when he sensed she'd refuse. Yeah, these were all tell-tale clues.

So far so good, she knew she was on the right track. But if true, what next? That left only one possibility; did she dare to even think about it? Did he want her so bad? Was it all planned? Did he desire her as much as she wanted him to? No, this was wishful thinking witch, wake-up!!! Still, the suspicion tantalised her, she toyed with the tendril of thought, with the idea, felt it, watched it until it dissolved like a stream of Tabasco in Lemon Crush.

She suddenly felt stupid, insecure; didn't she get what she wanted? A roll in the hay, but was that all or was she chasing a mirage? An illusion? She knew she had to get it over with, she'd confront him, not directly, or he'd clam up. She'd find a way . . . Phew, give it up for now witch, she was there, jumped out, cheerful, excited, apprehensive, and impatient; hugged him tight.

'Oh Baby', he grabbed her satchel, she was in his arms; he nuzzled her below the ear.

She quivered with delight; pressed herself tightly onto him; 'Quick Chris, take me now.'

'First the grub, Baby'

'No please', she begged, 'hurry.'

'No way, you've to eat.'

They entered the Mercearia Vencedora; she'd have been happy with a pasta and coke but he pushed her towards the breakfast buffet: Pequeno almoco, loaded her with ovas mexidos, rodela de batata, milho and tomate grelhado.

She protested, moaned, cried; it didn't work, well, might as well go along with it.

He forced her to eat, filled her up till she felt she'd burst, resembled a fat porco prior to Christmas Eve, he was relentless, 'C'mon baby, finish your grub.'

She gulped down her milk shake, 'Any particular reason, Chris?'

He smiled, 'Lots of work Baby.'

She blushed, kept her head down, and mumbled, 'Okey-Dokey.'

Follow up with Danish pastry and Compota de fruta Chocolate shake and coffee and they were out.

2 - SOFIA

They raced to the apartment, her 6th sense active, her brain into hyper-drive, she could sense the electricity crackling between them, the thinly disguised sense of urgency, was it her or was it him, she wondered.

He unlocked, then kicked the door open; thought this happened only in movies; words were once again unnecessary, unwanted, he devoured her, lips locked, lifted her, sneakers were perfunctorily kicked off, his hands were busy, no gentle probes this time, ripped her tees off.

'Wow!' He noticed her puppies supported by a La Perla push-up bra, raspberries erect!

'I draw First Blood', she smiled, 'get ready to die Chris.'

'Don't take it off', he begged and unbuttoned her jeans; down they went, she displayed the Tomahawk for the kill.

He was speechless, eyes wide, owlish, mesmerised, like a rabbit caught in the glare of car lamps.

She was happy, very happy, gave a silent prayer, 'Thank you Carriwell Lace Stretch, you've done your job.'

He was still frozen, stunned, like he'd had a blow in the solar plexus.

'Like it?'

'Don't Baby', his voice shook.

She pouted; and then twirled, 'Chris - am I hot?'

That did it; she felt her spine crack; 'Ask and It Will Be Given,' Matthew 7:7; she'd asked for it -in spades!!!

His grip was fierce, his hands shook (note it witch!!!), he ached with longing; his forearms shook.

She was expectant, vibrated with desire, his hand wrapped her hair around his forearm, was this a method, probably taught in Public School? He jerked her head back viciously, his tongue probed her ears; she shivered; and then it was just a red mist.

Their lips were busy, to make up for lost time, he chewed them, paused, she knew what for, her tongue darted out, shyly, he sucked; like a dying man would, for a glass of water in the desert; long and hard.

Cripes - That hurt. 'Mmmmm..mmmmm,' she tried to lodge a protest, he wouldn't let go; give it up witch, think something else. Her thoughts wandered, parallel processing again; men had serial, which is why they were so dumb, emotionally and intellectually handicapped . . .and easy; that's cruel witch, she chided herself, recollect how you whimpered and cried a week ago? Oh shut-up that was then, this is now, and like they say, revel in the NOW; she knew she had him, hook, line and sinker.

He'd paused. Wake up witch, he wants something. Why was he so freakin' tall? She was on her toes, hands around his neck, but could only manage to thrust her raisins into his belly button; his hands cupped her butt, lifted her, her legs high in the air, he pulled her one leg with his hand, she understood, wrapped herself around his waist, much better; he carried her to the bed, their breaths shallow.

She was on the pillow, looked at him - quizzed with her eyebrows 'What?'

He smiled, peeled his clothes off, she couldn't keep her

gaze away; he was big, getting bigger.

She tucked her thumbs on the waistband of her panties, he shook his head, she understood, kept them on, 'there go 40 Euros', she thought.

He went in the bath for a moment, came back covered, though she wouldn't mind having his baby; now hold on witch, hold on! What was that?

She broke her reverie, could feel his heat, he gripped her hand, was on top of her, guided her hand to his shaft, was she expected to put it in?

She grasped him.

'Move it Baby', what did he mean? She was in another world, her face wet with perspiration, flushed red; to breathe was difficult, her lips were wet, parted.

He'd said something, no freakin' use; she couldn't hear a word, nothing registered, he jerked her hand to show her, slight frown, impatience on his face; she understood.

Never criticise, her mother would say, now it was her turn to enter zombie-land; her wrists were thin but strong, she jerked the shaft till it grew, she forced herself to concentrate.

'Here comes trouble', she thought, 'on-time as ordered.'

'Okay, guide it in Baby', he whispered.

She recovered her senses with effort, stay on track witch and confront him now, in his moment of desire, when he was weak.

'Chris, could we talk about it?' she hesitated, 'please?'

'Later Baby', he said, 'first take the edge-off.'

'Off what?'

'The hunger, Baby.'

Weird, cryptic, 'Chris, do you want me?' she teased while her hand coaxed and guided the shaft to the edge of her sweet-box; she'd pulled her legs wide, she was ready.

'Always and forever.'

Another tell; she thought, his mouth covered hers, her chest crushed under his weight, he moved inside her, took it slow, waited for her to loosen up.

She felt wet, wild and wonderful; it hurt, yes, a sort of dull ache, where the bruises were. It hit her than, like a thunderbolt, OMG so this was what it was all about.

He was completely in, she felt tight, filled.

'Chris', she whispered hoarsely, 'is this sex?'

'Uh-huh', he was busy, started to move, increased the pace, pulled her ankles and joined them behind his back.

This was freakin' crazy, the pace increased, he hammered her, like a train, her head banged against the bed-rest, skull knocked on wood, stop freakin'-out witch, wake-up. No, to concentrate was impossible, her mind wandered, some noise in the background, squeals of a cat? No, a porco more likely.

A porco? Regular squeals, of torture? Couldn't say, it was strange, she hadn't noticed any pets in the house. Who kept Porcos for pets anyway? Had she finally lost it? Strained to listen, muffled, rhythmic, coincided with . . . her? No Way!

Yes Way!!!It was her! Never dreamt it possible, did you witch? Can't you freakin' shut-up? This was, crazy, her squeals and rhythm matched his thrusts. Thank Goodness he'd covered her mouth. Was it deliberate? To mute the freakin' audio of a porn queen (porn queen huh?) on full volume!!!

It was time for Liftoff, can't think, his hand against her head, to soften the banging on her skull, the other below her butt, could feel him, was it possible, for him to go in deeper? And deeper, this was insane, she was blowing her mind, she arched, every muscle fibre tense, the thrusts, unrelenting, pushed even further.

Her nails, on his back, pierced skin, she was in

dreamland, possessed by the Devil, 'Harder', her command a whisper, he complied, it was unbearable, she wanted to scream and scream and scream.

'Almost there', shrieks of endearment, 'amante!'

Who was that? Was that you, witch? No, it was the Devil; call the freakin' exorcist, Chris, like Right Now!!!

Wilder and wilder, her mouth demanding, neck muscles taut, it was NOW, she sobbed, couldn't hold it any longer, her back arched further, lifted him, long shallow moan, shuddered, every muscle fibre taut, body vibrated with electricity and then . . .

It was over, not in one happy event like the books said, but shudders, 9 on the Richter Scale, then lower and lower and lower till she was loose, her body limp, a waterfall and then she'd turned into a rag doll.

He arrived a few minutes later, kept at it till he was empty; she felt hot lava all the way in.

'Leave it in', she whispered.

He panted, perspired, his heartbeat the thud of a train engine.

Gave her half-a-minute . . . then, 'I'm up Baby', he slipped out, 'get you some grub.'

'Not me', she moaned, 'please, Chris, let me sleep.'

'Kay', he slipped out, got up, took a step ahead then turned back to look, stopped abruptly to stare, mesmerised by the vision. Her skin glowed red, her hair was disheveled, the undergarments askew if not ripped to shreds, legs sprawled all over the place, sheets wet, lips parted, her chest heaved as her breathing returned to normal, hair aflame, flecks of foam caught on the entrance to her glistening sweet-box.

'Aphrodite', he whispered, in complete awe.

She heard. 'No Chris', she mumbled, eyes closed, 'Sofia - I've tasted the Forbidden Fruit.'

3 - TRAIN KEPT A ROLLIN'

An eternity later, it was time to surface; she got up, went to the bath, looked at herself, wake up sleepy head, she was exhausted, no wonder he stuffed her up every time.

Gentle knock on the door, now what? She cringed, not that, not again.

'It's not locked.'

'Nothing Baby', he said, 'I've got the grub.'

'Kay', what was the flamin' hurry anyway? Don't be dense, witch; you know what you're here for, yeah, she giggled, brushed her hair. A woman's hair reflects her mind, poor Chris could wait.

Poor Chris? What had happened to her? Where did that come from? She looked another, closer look at herself; nothing discernable, nothing physical, but, once again, she sensed the change. She felt powerful, elated, wonderful, is this what making love could do? Making love? Her memory came alive, yes; she had her answer - why they called it making love.

She was out, checked out the tray; hmm nicely laid out . . . Glasses of fresh juice, Lemon Crush, cheese, crackers, chunks of fish, some kind of pastry and vinho.

She gorged herself, no prompting this time, he poured her some juice; 'what for Chris?' she mumbled between mouthfuls.

'To prevent dehydration', he said.

Cryptic again, let it go, drink up, God, she was thirsty, nibbled the cheese, he waited for her to finish, picked up the dishes and turned.

She gasped; there were two rhythmic scars etched on the sides of his back, streaks of red, thin trails of clotted blood.

It was fresh. She was horrified, 'Chris what happened? Did you hurt yourself? Who did this?'

'One guess', he said dryly.

Her mouth dropped, 'No, no, this is terrible', she wanted to touch, the lacerations were wet, her eyes were moist, how could she, was she crazy? She deserved to be locked up.

'I'm ever so sorry', she begged, 'can I make up for it Chris?'

She caught the sudden change in his body, he was thoughtful, eager, pulled her close, looked into her eyes; it was the child, honest, open, curious, 'Yes Baby', he whispered, 'know what a Honey Scrub is?'

She shook her head - No. Now concentrate witch!!!

'D'u know what's a facial?'

'Er . . . yes', she said shyly, she'd prepared herself for this, 'it's when you cum over my . . . '

'Exactly', he cut her off, 'this is the reverse, but there's something more.'

She waited; he'd stopped, was thinking, her raisins started to quiver, a shiver of delight ran up her legs, 'Chris, tell me,' she encouraged, 'I owe you this time.' Funny witch, look who's talking.

'Can I drink you Baby?'

She blushed; look at Yoda, The Wise One. Dumb witch,

what was that? Figure it out later; just say yes, she smiled, 'What are we waiting for?'

He took the tray away, came back with towels to place them on the bed, turned, lay on his back, gingerly, 'don't worry about the scratches, they'll heal, let's get on with it.'
She was puzzled.
'C'mon Baby.'
What did he mean? She climbed over his stomach; 6-pack she noted, with approval; looked down, he smiled, his hands were over her butt, 'I'll guide you' he said, and pulled her over his face.
She understood, lowered herself down, ouch, she jumped; it was like stepping on a naked wire, a freakin' electric shock, her cherry was sensitive, she was damp, she sensed his lips trying to locate her p-hole, he did, it was in his mouth.
'Now Baby', he mumbled, hands tightened over her butt.
What now? She was confused; he said he wanted to drink her???To drink? Literally? At least that's what she thought, with the way she was positioned it meant only one thing; she was again losing it; or was she? Look into his eyes for a clue, no, they were closed, she sensed his impatience, she tensed up, screw it! Let it happen.
The jet-stream slammed the back of his throat, he drank greedily, she was still shy, started to withdraw, his hands stopped her, 'enough champagne', he smiled, 'time for nectar.'
Champagne, huh? Great - nectar what? Her silky red-brown hair was just above his lips, she stared, what could he mean? Wake-up witch, she felt thick-headed! Follow his lead, he pushed her, she moved, slow, awkward at first; she gripped the headboard for balance, okay, understood, he'd

called it the honey-scrub, she increased her pace.

'Careful Baby', he mumbled, 'my nose.'

This was fun, 'know something Chris?'

'mm hmmm.'

'I'm really enjoying this.'

it was hard-work, she started to perspire, felt hot, was soaked, already; his face glistened, his hands on her butt felt warm, pleasant; she had an idea, stopped, 'Chris, turn aside', wow, are you calling the shots, witch???

He looked puzzled, turned.

She resumed, he was slick with her, she stopped again, he took the cue, turned, she was in control, back again, chin, nose, forehead, back.

'Speed-it-up Baby', he mumbled.

Beads of perspiration trickled down her arms, she was glad lucky she was athletic; this required flexibility as well as coordination; she made a quick mental note, check Honey Scrub with Cintia; she was sure she'd draw a blank there as well. So far so good, but this was one-way street; she was going out of control, losing it too fast, her thighs tightened, this was THE BIG ONE, she increased the pace, tensed up, her body shuddered, she was early, but it was impossible to wait, any more and she'd lose control, it had to be now.

His hands held her rigid, stopped, surprised; his open mouth took her, cum hit the back of his throat, sure he wanted this? Could it be? Too late, can't stop, she went on and on. Phew! He'd closed his mouth over her sweet-box, nevertheless, she pushed herself in, as hard as she could, emptied, stopped.

He chided her, 'What did you stop for?'

'I . . . ,' she was nonplussed, felt dumb, didn't know what to say, she was empty, didn't he know she was empty?

He was impatient, 'C'mon Baby, I'm thirsty.'

Okay, here we go again, she was excited, this felt good.

'Faster', he mumbled.

She looked down, he was nestled under her hair, wet - or soaked - she wondered if he really liked it. She keep at it, slow this time, long strokes, his hands behind her butt, increased pressure, she was hot, sweaty, her steady raindrops of perspiration made a mess of his hair.

It was time, 'Ready?' She whispered; she held herself for a moment and then - Wham!!! It was over.

He mumbled, from deep down, 'more.'

She felt stupid, helpless, 'I can't.'

He looked up; did he appear disappointed - or desperate? It was strange, she'd never seen that look on his face before; it was a tell.

'Okay, wait.' She flopped down on the pillows, the great disconnect, she was drained, but there was a way; she gripped her cherry between the leaves with both fingers.

'What's this Baby?'

She was puzzled, didn't he know, 'It's how I . . . '

'All wrong, it's very tender, you'll damage the nerves', he said gently, 'listen, keep your hands where they are and turn.'

She rolled over, waited.

'Okay, move, like this', his hands pushed her - first up then down.

She caught on, 'I've got it.'

He waited.

Eyes closed, embarrassed, can't refuse, rhythm increased, moments later, she felt it, 'mm almost there', tried to warn him, to get ready.

'Wait', he slipped under her, 'now', caught her in his mouth, 'mmm pure nectar, nice Baby, now turn', he mumbled.

4 - COUGAR

She did, he got busy, she was exhausted; live and learn, she couldn't wait to tell Cintia; closed her eyes, felt his lips, fingers, inside, he was busy, why, with what? Yeah, this was a tell alright. It was unusual, she'd never heard about it anywhere; yes, it was apparent that he wanted something, but what? Don't dream or speculate, this was important, but more important was - Why?

He continued to probe, incessant, demanding, had found a hidden valve, gentle pressure, released a torrent she didn't know existed, she couldn't take it anymore, bucked.

'Ooow, my nose.'

'Sorry Chris', dazed, emptied out, she was soaked like never before. What was this? She had to know, curious, asked him 'Chris, how do you do it?' No - that wasn't it, she'd meant to ask - Why!

'More.'

'I'm empty Chris', though he tried to hide, she'd caught his disappointed look, he tried to change but it was too late; she knew then that something bothered him and it ran deep, but what it was would have to be found out.

But that was for later, she shook herself awake, she was

alert, 'Is there another way Chris?' she asked helpfully.

Yes there was, though he didn't say, but she caught the hope in his eyes, it was like a sudden burst of sunlight on a cloudy day; he was silent, though, looked almost embarrassed; she watched - it was the strongest emotion she'd seen since the day he broke down.

She had to encourage him, 'Oh c'mon Chris', she chided, 'we're lovers now', that was sly, witch, smart of her to slip it in, what had he to say to that?

Did he notice? Said quietly, 'there is a way,' his tone betrayed him, almost as if he expected her to refuse.

'Trust me', she was disappointed, didn't he notice, what she'd called them? Lovers. It revealed the depth of his preoccupation, 'I'm not a child anymore Chris, trust me', she repeated.

Sunny smile at last, 'Okay', he leapt up, 'back in a moment.'

She sighed, this was weird, crazy, but she knew she was on to something – for one thing, he was thirsty all the time; for her, she giggled; and was the Honey Scrub important or what came after? Plus why did refer to cum as nectar?

The look of disappointment on his face was REAL, by any standard, she hadn't imagined the whole thing; her 6th sense told her that there was something more to it, but what?

No one there to trade notes with; she'd ask him, but would he answer? Or deliberately brush her off? The latter was more likely, he'd never answer directly, she'd have to work it around somehow, her brain worked on the sidelines; for example, lately she owed him for the scratches, but what if he owed her? Marilyn vos Savant might have an IQ of 228 but she was equally, if not better, competent; a path through the darkness glimmered in the forest of her brain. . .

'Here', he was back, handed her a carton of milk, the top off, was she supposed to drink? He was busy screwing around somewhere, arranging a fresh towel under her pelvis; this was definitely crazy.

She took a sip, 'I'm not the one who's thirsty Chris', puzzled, 'you are.'

He was back down, 'go on, pour', he peeled her open, waited.

She caught on, 'you mean. . .?' And moved the carton to her sweet-box.

'C'mon Baby', he nodded, 'all of it.'

She had to see!!!

'Chris, can I watch?'

She didn't wait for a reply but raised her knees, slowly and poured the milk down, cascading down her cherry to the sweet-box into his mouth, spilling from the sides onto the towel; this was a fantastic turn on if ever there was one!!!

She slowly emptied the carton out; she watched the rivulets cascade down her sides; his mouth, his throat, the look of satisfaction on his face. . .

She tensed up, a switch had been turned-on, was this why they called it a turn-on; no reason to get alarmed witch, or was there? Her feelings were confused, what was going on? Her hand stopped, paused, of its own accord?

He looked up, noticed, her eyes were glazed, hooded, he knew, understood in a flash, leapt up to prepare himself.

For a mindless instant she wanted to hurt him; no reason at all, a sudden understanding of a well-guarded secret electrified her brain, the reason for her cruelty, translated into primitive, sexual urge, nothing more nothing less. . .

She was terrified, held him tightly, tried to hold on to her sanity, moaned softly, 'I don't want to hurt you, Chris', lying witch, she wanted to do exactly that!!!

He entered her in a flash, words were unnecessary, his mouth covered hers, a part of her tasted milk, another part dug her nails behind his back, teeth on his lips, she bit into the soft yielding fruit - it was for her, an offering, a sacrifice for the Goddess . . .

He acted as if he knew, he murmured, 'Don't hold back Baby.'

Her mouth filled with the heady taste of blood, it was addictive, she moaned, wanted more.

'Let go, Sweetheart, I know, I'm there', he said.

She didn't know who she was; or maybe she knew only too well; a shape-shifting Goddess; a nocturnal carnivorous feminine , transposed to another reality; and he - just another mass of flesh, created for her pleasure, owned by her, his sole purpose of existence - to be mauled by her lust.

Three-quarters of an hour later,

'C'mon Baby,' his voice far away, hands gently prised hers, no use, her hands hid her face, red, embarrassed, she couldn't face him, it was over, she'd go back and try to forget about it.

'C'mon Angie,' he was gentle, 'look at me.'

She wouldn't, just wanted to sink in the ground, couldn't bear to look, she was no good, an animal, she should be in a zoo, or would that be cruelty to animals? No . . . she had to be locked up, committed . . .

'Nothing wrong in what you did.'

Surprise!!! She heard him; detected the humour in his voice; was it possible he'd forgiven her?

'A Scorpion female usually kills her mate after making love.'

She mumbled, 'I'm not a scorpion Chris.'

'We'll discuss that later,' he smiled, 'and, incidentally, you have blood on your hands.'

She didn't move. 'Go away Chris, I'm too ashamed to look.'

He grinned, 'Then don't. Ride the Snake instead.'

'Ride the . . .?'

'Uh huh, face away, I want to see your butt.'

Her curiosity aroused, she opened her eyes, evaded his, he was ready, 'Chris, first forgive me.'

'You'll be forgiven,' he smiled, 'only when you climb up.'

She perked up, smiled, 'Okay, what next?'

Too embarrassed to look at him, she turned towards his feet, held him, confused.

'Climb-on Baby', he whispered.

She did, slowly, easily, winced, it was in, wedged tight.

'Ride.'

She waited, took a deep breath, sank down, till she was filled; waited to get damp, time to move, started, awkward at first, settled in, it felt different; Thank God for strong thighs; she placed her hands on his legs, felt his tension, his body was taut, smiled, look who's in control now, it was better, there was a response from her, she was slick, it'd became easier, her mind wandered, where did it go? Was she so elastic, look down, 'I can see you twitch', she giggled.

He moaned, 'Faster Baby.'

No more fun and games, go for it, time to increase the pace, careful, keep him inside, bounce, look who's damp, it was the Zombie, but who? Her or Him? Or both?

She wanted to express herself, vocally, cry out, say something, it was strenuous, took effort, perspiration streamed down her back, the rhythm was set, she vibrated like steel, on the edge, now, now, now, he shuddered, raised himself up, she felt the heat inside, molten lava, he was shrinking, twisted her legs, tight, to keep him, timed it till she came with a gush, a moan, a shudder and trembled back to normal.

She was soaked, kept sitting, to get her breath back; took her time, wait a few more seconds, get up, let him out, gently, looked back, he smiled, called her, what now?

'Uh huh, c'mon before you dry up, Baby', he said, 'every drop is precious.'

Great, live and learn!

He held her soaked body, soft, warm, pliable, licked her perspiration dry, wherever it flowed, droplets of salt, armpits, back of knees, sucked her toes, licked the thin film of fresh sweat off her, it tickled her, she liked it, for a moment, blushed, twitched, 'isn't it dirty Chris.'

'Not to a man dying of thirst.'

Another tell!!! She had all the weapons she needed, to skin him, but that was later.

He was back at it, persistent, then finished, 'I'm kaput Baby', he smiled, 'have a shower, I'll get lunch.'

She nodded, smiled - Wow! Was she exhausted; this was crazy, weird, wild and wonderful; tried to get up, her thighs shook, held onto the wall, few steps, okay, better, walk to the bath, look at the mirror; who was this creature? Dried streaks of blood between her teeth, chin and chest, impish smile, hair disarray, even Cintia wouldn't recognise her; she was Wolverine's sister; she brushed her teeth, turned the tap on, gentle, warm jets of water hit her skin, mind was a blank, funny, never felt this way before, 'coz you never did this before.

She smiled as she washed the flecks of dried blood from

her fingertips; didn't know why, or for what; she felt in control, the part of her brain, segregated from the rest, given the sole task of cornering him had said something; she'd thought of a way to break him, just had to take it super-slow; it was important, her 6th sense told her, but how and why was still a freakin' mystery.

5 - ISIS

They were in bed, together; she was delirious, crazed with joy, she'd dreamt of it, so often, it was always a wet dream; the love cycle; make love–clean-up – eat - recharge – back to work; couldn't wait to tell Cintia.

She lazed in his arms, he fed her gently, lovingly, fruit flavoured yogurt, cheese, sandwiches, pizza, eggs, juice, an early makeshift microwave lunch, lovers only, could she market that? She'd try.

He was pre-occupied, time to get him back, offer him bits of grape, on her tongue, into his mouth, the juices leaked down her chin; he'd lick it off, she caught on quick; deliberately dropped mango and pineapple slices between her breasts, on her tummy, into her belly button, and . . . should she???No, wait, she giggled.

He raised an eyebrow, 'Naughty thoughts, Baby?'
She nibbled pear, 'Thinking of us.'
He smiled, kissed her cheek, 'I know I'm a bother.'
'C'mon Chris', she blushed, 'never say that again.'

Why oh why couldn't she be Miss Cool; one reason, she still hadn't forgotten how she'd mauled him, couldn't look him in the face, he had two crescent shaped circles on his poor bruised swollen lips; with tiny teeth marks, of a raccoon. . . or a wildcat!!!

His neck was scratched through, she didn't dare look at his back, she was ashamed, wanted to make up for her behavior, her hand wandered down, felt him, limp, stroked.

'No use Baby', he shrugged wryly, 'I'm a corpse.'

This was her chance, she thought fast.

'You know a lot Chris', she squeezed, 'but you don't know me', she said, encouraged him, 'you CAN get it up.'

'Uh huh, never', he smiled, 'I know when I'm done.'

'Wanna bet?' She grinned, 'up and running in 10 minutes?'

'Take 15, but it's over.'

'C'mon', impatiently, 'what do I get?'

'Anything Baby.'

Impish smile,' Anything?'

'Anything.'

'Okay then, I'll ask only ONE thing Chris', her eyes hopeful, 'Will you answer me truthfully?'

He tried to look innocent,' about what Baby?'

'C'mon Chris, don't pretend', she caught on, 'only one question?'

'K, Baby', he relented, lay back, closed his eyes, 'but let's see the magic first'; deep within, he knew she could.

'Here I go.'

She bounced up happily, knew what to do, she thought, this was easy.

He was in her mouth, limp, warm, she wasn't in a hurry, worked on him lazily; one hand stroked the root, saw him twitch, the other nudged the shaft, her tongue worked the head, blind eye, the drawstring; she started to daydream, her thoughts far away; she had time, but till when?

With her grades she could slide into Pamplin Business School easily, where her sister was, she wanted a GSB qualification; though fat lot of good it'd do in the slowdown; but then she'd have to leave Lisboa.

And what about Chris, could she live without him? Stupid question, she wanted to be with him, that much was certain, then why leave?

To get away from prying eyes, no more subterfuge. But would they let her, that was the question, or more importantly, would she want to? Would she see him there? No.

Oh, screw it, enjoy the moment.

He stirred, she was getting there; her thoughts rambled on; why was she so confident about this and not herself? Especially when he was around? She was head over heels in . . . No, she wouldn't use that 4-letter word, it had a variety of undertones, she didn't want to trap him; she felt stupid and confused.

Time to switch over: what was it with him? Why was he The Sphinx? That's unfair, witch, when did I ever get time to ask him, OK, but couldn't he have let me know; about how he feels, for me? Why now, in bits and pieces, when we do it, why make me wait? Yeah, witch, and what would he have said? 'I like your butt?' And that too in front of your mother, right? That'd be really neat.

Time to wake-up witch!!!If he'd told you, would you've ever bothered about studies? Kept a good score?

Yeah, sobering thought, but what did she want now? She hated tradition, always had, unlike Cintia, who always whined for a relationship. That's cruel witch, easy to say when you have a rock-steady relationship; but was Rock-Steady right?

Dead meat's getting warmer by the minute; she rhymed - the snake will wake, she pushed her thoughts on the backburner, concentrate now; she worked on him furiously, small bites, nibbles, teased, stroked, kept him wet, just like he wanted.

Why did he made her drink juices and stuff; and then drink her? Hee hee, she couldn't giggle. Never mind, she'd know soon enough.

Wow!!! This was magic; she was a sorceress!!! Her mouth quickly filled up, she nursed him a little more; and – voila!!! She leaned back, exhausted.

She'd achieved the impossible, he was up, solid, quivered, wet, dripped, he felt it, felt her power, his spine shivered, his senses aflame, he knew she could, his eyes were closed, he was afraid, did he dare look?

'C'mon Chris, I've won', victory, child-like voice, impatient, 'you owe me!!!' She looked at her handiwork; a musical score would be great; she was the Goddess of Wisdom, Renewal and Reincarnation.

'You'll get what you want', he said, 'but first things first.'

She knew what he implied, but let's tease some; make him wait, make him sweat, she giggled, 'no Chris', first talk to me.'

'Please Baby', he moaned.

His hand picked up a bottle olive oil, extra virgin, from the salad tray, she was curious, 'what's that for, Chris?'

'Turn around', he said slowly, 'on your hands and knees, you know Baby.'

Oh No, Not THAT again!!! 'No Chris,' she begged, 'I'm not in the mood.'

'Please baby,' he pleaded, 'for me?'

She felt the heat of his desire, his eyes locked onto hers, again that haunted look, like as if almost expected her to refuse; but could she really? Never, she knew she'd regret it later, but that was later, the moment was now!!! She felt sorry for him, smiled her acceptance. . . 'Anything for you, my darling,' was it wasted on him? Didn't he notice her terms of endearment?

She turned around slowly, got ready.

His fingers were busy, excited, explored her, she felt the olive oil, the sensation was not unpleasant, but she'd rather not if she had a choice; no way out now, might as well go through the freakin' torture.

He fidgeted some more, her head yanked up; he was sliding in too fast, the pain was sharp, she gasped weakly 'it hurts . . . so much,' she protested; he was in, another pause, and then a full thrust, there was little resistance, she kept her back fully arched, moaned.

He gripped her butt, firm, balanced, sculpted, he got harder by the minute, she held him tightly, enveloped him, completely, he'd stopped.

Her spine was not right, he tapped, 'lower Baby', she did, the pain was over, must've touched a nerve, she could relax, but only slightly.

He stopped, stared, she was wonderful; a Living Goddess, a work of art.

She turned, impatient, 'C'mon Chris.'

'Sorry Baby', he said, 'just admiring the architecture', started to move.

She was excited, glad, tried to maintain her balance, the zombie stage would be rough, she was prepared, he increased the pace, he was hummed with pleasure; well at least someone's happy.

Zombie's arrived, she tried to look, couldn't, her elbows folded, her head fell on the pillow, eyes shut tight, where am I, not a creature of this earth, she was a shape-shifting goddess, her head knocked on wood, whoever lived below wouldn't have to exercise their brain too much; to guess what was happening upstairs.

She hadn't yet explored the house fully, knew there were two baths and an alcove with a window for the kitchen; these were for singles; but she wouldn't mind, moving in;

wake up witch, this is not part of the script! Yeah, neither was her aching fudge chute.

Sweat streamed down his body, he was panting, breathless, almost there, she was tight, terrific, it was time, his spine curved, as did hers, excited him further, the final phase - he slammed her, viciously, couldn't help, would apologise later, she was irresistible.

He came, deep inside, molten lava, hot and wet; she stiffened with the shock, squeezed him tight, no idea how she knew, but she did, had she done it before? Possibly in another world, another galaxy but not in this freakin' lifetime; felt him shudder, didn't expect that, did you Lover? He was taken aback, the surprise was complete.

It was over, her legs sprawled, she fell, he was on top of her, quickly supported himself on elbows, gentle soft kisses, nibbles, her ears, cheeks, eyes, forehead, murmurs, whispers, terms of endearment, of gratefulness, almost a litany, he collapsed, exhausted, careful not to crush her.

He didn't pull out, was too exhausted.

Wow! She'd pulverised him! This was power; there was no time to think, her lungs worked overtime, concentrate, recover your breath, perspiration mingled, bodies were locked into each other, the dance of life was over, they were eternally entwined, or so it seemed.

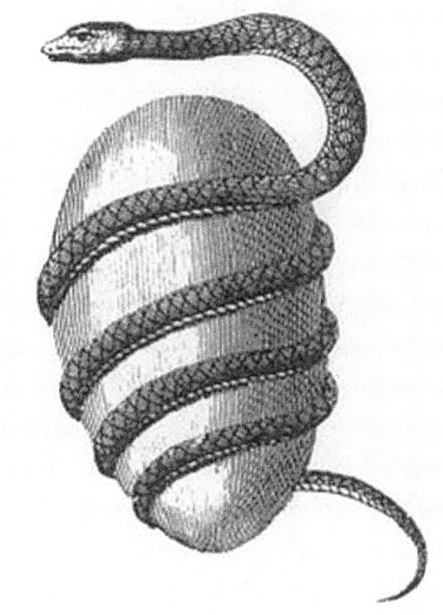

III - NECTAR OF IMMORTALITY

1 - MICHAEL DOUGLAS

Time to clean-up; his obsession with hygiene was another clue; he didn't want a Michael DOUGLAS. She was in the bath; he - in the kitchen. Why did he think he had to beef her up all the time? Phew, concentrate witch - she poured some soap-gel, rubbed it all over, was careful with her hair as there'd be no time to fix it later; her mind schemed overtime, how do I break The Sphinx?

Knock on the door.

'Come in', she liked that, he never invaded her privacy, even though she told him to.

He said, 'Ready for tea?' and stopped to stare.

She caught the look, 'No way Chris', she said, 'Not now.'

'What a waste', he murmured.

'Later', she smiled.

A tray, tea-time, lemonade, cake and crisps, back on bed, she shielded herself with a pillow, busy eating, God; she was hungry; whereas he lived on air . . . and her; she giggled.

He smiled, 'Anything, Baby?' concerned.

'Chris,' she had to remind him, 'you promised.'

'I know Baby', he looked at the clock.

'We'll have time.'

He was surprised.

'I can read your mind, Chris.'

'I know.' '

He nibbled her ear, tongue inside.

'That tickles Chris!!!Stop', she giggled, 'I get distracted.'

'Don't talk when you eat, Baby', he chided gently.

She swallowed, 'I wanna talk.'

'K Baby', he was smiling, 'don't turn me on then.'

'Don't make me', she said.

He stared right inside her soul, if that was possible, she blushed, kept her head down, was disconcerted, stupid witch, why feel shy, why NOW!!!Wake up witch, this couldn't wait, careful how you do it; remember not to be direct.

She began, 'Do you remember the movie "Silence of the Lambs" Chris? We saw it together, you know.'

'Uh huh.'

'I was 8 then. And you shielded my eyes most of the time.'

'To save you from the gory details.'

'Yes, but then I got so mad', she smiled, 'I watched it a zillion times to see what you wanted to hide.'

He smiled, she was leading him somewhere, but what? Play along.

'Do you remember the scene where Anthony Hopkins is caged and Jodie Foster questions him?'

He knew something was coming, 'What about it?'

'Anthony Hopkins tells her the murders were incidental; the killer covets being a woman.'

'Uh huh.'

'So, what I mean to ask you is', she stammered, 'wh-wh-what do you covet, Chris?'

She stared, her eyes soft, cajoled, she'd pinned him; he was cornered, trapped; no way out now.

'Am I right Chris', she felt sorry for him, but she had to know, 'making love is incidental, right?'

He was quiet for a while, and then gently, 'Why do you say that, Baby?'

'Easy Chris', she said, 'you can't wait to go down.'

'No big deal; and?'

'Michael DOUGLAS scares you.'

'Anyone would be; and?'

He was smart, but she had a trump card, 'The look on your face', she reminded him.

'What about it?'

'It's a tell!!!'

'A . . . what?'

'A tell', she was impatient; 'Teen-speak for "you slipped"; my turn now Chris.'

He was quiet for a long time; a far-away look in his eyes, 'You're partially right and partially wrong, Baby.'

'Uh huh.'

'Making love is not incidental, he struggled to speak, 'but yes, the rest is true.'

Phew!!!She was so freakin' relieved!!! 'Maybe I can help you Chris', she coaxed him, 'try me.'

He was silent, his eyes faraway, she had to bring him back; some humour would do it; she knew what. 'Do you know what David ICKE says about the British Royal Family?'

'No', he stared at her; taken aback; dumbfounded.

'He says they are descended from lizards ', she continued, 'because they have pop-out eyes.'

He stared blankly.

'So, please don't worry Chris', she coaxed him, I'm sure it isn't as weird as that.'

He was silent, didn't look at her.

It was her turn to get worried, 'or is it?'

'No Baby', he shook his head, 'you surprised me, that's all.'

'Then tell me', she repeated, 'what do you covet?'

Should he or shouldn't he? He resigned himself; she had a right to know, after all, she was The Source.

'The Nectar of Immortality', he replied.

She was stunned, didn't expect that did you, Witch! Her turn to be silent! She took a deep breath, 'and you really think I', she was tongue-tied, couldn't say what she thought continued, 'have it?'

He stared back, 'Yes', his face frank and open, 'but I'm not the only one.'

'Who else?'

'Acharya S; when she talks about the Temple Goddesses; she says, quote "their very secretions were supposed to have medical virtue ." unquote'

'I don't get it Chris', she shook her head, 'can you explain?'

'It's not easy', he said, 'it has to be understood'

'What Chris?'

'The concept . . . '

'I'm ready Chris', she interrupted.

'. . . of the Divine Feminine, how it originated, what it means.'

'Wow', this was great stuff; she thought as she settled back, hugged the pillow, 'go ahead.'

Nectar of Immortality, huh, she waited while Chris groped for words to begin.

'Ancient mythology talks about The Divine Feminine, viz Goddesses who possess the Nectar of Immortality.'

'What's the big deal?'

'Only Kinky Sex could release the Nectar; Or the lack of it.'

'Give me an example Chris.'

'Well, 'kay, Rusalka is the water nymph in Czech mythology', he said, 'with skin the colour of moonlight.'

'Good for her.'

'And Vila is her rival', he continued, 'she's blonde, flighty and has an affinity to fire; and both these Goddesses have something in common.'

'They have the Nectar?'

'You guessed it Baby', he smiled, 'They are Virgin Fairies with seductive power over men, but check out the difference in the way they act – While Kinky Sex is applicable to Rusalka, Vila makes them dance till dawn till they die of exhaustion at daybreak.'

'Horrifying!!!'

'The death or not getting it', he smiled.

She threw a pillow at him, 'C'mon Chris!!!'

'Okay, okay, here we go', he said, 'the Kelts believe that Kinky Sex leads to God Realisation.'

'Uh huh.'

'Kelts believed the female body was sacred, inasmuch it contained the building blocks of life.'

'And what are they?'

'That's the debate', he said, 'if you still remember your Life Sciences class; what is the basic ingredient the body cannot do without?'

'Carbon?'

'Carbon constitutes 18% of the body, but no. In fact, 96% of the human body consists of just four elements - Oxygen, Carbon, Hydrogen and Nitrogen. We know the importance of Oxygen, but Nitrogen deficiency, or an amino acid deficiency can kill. Nitrogen at 3% in the human body is used to build Amino Acids, DNA, RNA and proteins; Nitrogen also facilitates growth and maintenance, metabolism, muscle growth and runs the biological clock.'

'Isn't there enough in the atmosphere?'

'Yes but the body can't absorb it directly', he said, 'One way is through sugar. Glucose is sweet, crystalline and contains one molecule of Nitrogen and two of Hydrogen. The Amino Acid tryptophan produces Tryptamine; all Nitrogen compounds end in –ine; and the Pineal Gland produces Di-Methyl-Tryptamine or DMT.'

2 - MOJO

'Rhymes with Nicotine.'

'Clever.' he mused, 'which is why smokers can't kick the habit.'

'Is that the last word Chris?'

'Absolutely;once you're hooked, you're hooked.'

'But why?'

'According to Rick STRASSMAN, MD, the brain hungers for DMT', he said. 'We can explore another possibility - that DMT is the Nectar of Immortality.'

'And where is it found, Chris?'

'Julius AXELROD , the Nobel Prize winning scientist of the US National Institute of Health found DMT in human tissue, urine and the Cerebro-Spinal Fluid which bathes the brain.'

'To deviate slightly', he continued, 'a fluid is also triggered by pressing the sweet-spot, or G-spot, as described by Lisa LONGHOFER', he continued, 'in fact, she wrote a book on it.'

'What does it do?'

'What we call cum, is released when aroused and may or may not contain DMT, although it is suspected to. The reasons are debatable but if not DMT, then one possibility would be to cool you down.'

'Didn't they test?'

'Yes; it contained higher levels of glucose than urine, and an enzyme; Prostatic Acid Phosphatase (PAP); which is characteristic of a major component of semen.'

'Semen in a woman's body?' She was surprised, 'how?'

'Not semen Baby; PAP. Research indicates that it's also a pain suppressant; and lasts longer than morphine, but that is a hypothesis until proven.'

'No wonder you're addicted.'

He smiled. 'In 1996, Mike CROWLEY published a paper titled "When the Gods Drank Urine." The subject is not similar, but related.'

'There's no shortage of weirdos in this world Chris', she said, 'but you're trying to reach somewhere – so go ahead.'

'I'll now include another hypothesis: If Kinky Sex can give you the Nectar of Immortality, can it also lead to God Realisation?'

'This is dangerous territory Chris,' she warned, 'you could be burnt at the stake.'

He was silent.

'Don't let me scare you, Chris', she continued, 'Coming back to "Kinky Sex leads to God Realisation"; do you think there's something more to it', she was hesitant, shy, her voice trailed off, 'you, me, us, what we did?'

'I'm getting there. First I want you to check-out a video in You Tube A Trip through the Water Door by Steve WILNER', he said. 'Water can be used to energise, to recharge, especially after a long hard day.'

'Like today?' she giggled.

'Pay attention now', he said, 'the Kelts perceived water as both creator and destroyer of life.'

'Really interesting', sounded familiar, she'd been this on

route before, shook her head, tried to remember, couldn't, 'go ahead Chris.'

'They also believed that groves, springs and pools were enchanted entrances to the other world', he continued, 'and we can connect to this world through Ether and Water.'

'What other world?'

'Isaac ASIMOV called the world we live in - the Tardyon Universe; a world limited by the Speed of Light i.e. now represented by the symbol c.'

She caught the emphasis, 'Was it different earlier?'

'Although c is now the universal symbol for the speed of light, the most common symbol in the nineteenth century was an upper-case V .'

She caught the intended meaning, 'OMG, Chris that's head-on!!!'

'We cross the Luzon Wall where everything is at c or V if you prefer', he smiled.

'And then?'

'Then there is the Tachyon Universe, where everything is greater than the Speed of Light.'

'C'mon Chris, that's Basic Physics', she chirped, glad at the fact that she could correct him. 'Nothing can exceed the Speed of Light.'

'Nothing can accelerate beyond the Speed of Light ', he corrected, 'which means sub-atomic particles in the Tachyon Universe exist beyond V.'

'Which also means Chris', she smiled, 'that Time and Space don't exist.'

His turn to be surprised!

'Wake up silly', she smiled. 'I read the entire Isaac ASIMOV collection in the library before I was 16.'

He was still stunned.

'Back on track, Chris', she asked quickly, 'Where do you get Ether?'

'The Sensation of Touch is Ether.'

She had him in her hand, gently stroked him, 'like this?' He was getting there, 'this is great stuff Chris, why can't we market this, together?'

'Like any new technology', he was back on top of her, 'it has to be ruthlessly tested first.'

'So would you like to connect', her wrist moved, to guide him, 'to the Tachyon Universe?'

'Uh huh,' he smiled, 'I want to scale the Luzon Wall.'

He was ready, and so was she.

'Please Chris,' she whispered, shyly, hands on his chest, 'can we go slow? I want this to last.'

3 - SELKET

They took a nap, legs entwined, arms sprawled about.

Her body ached, she was bruised but happy. As well as exhausted, empty, filled, satiated and spent. Her thoughts bounced inside her skull, what now, what next? There was something important, she struggled to remember, her memory was good, she recalled it, sat up, shook him awake.

'Chris, don't chicken out now', she wouldn't let him slip away this time for sure. 'Who is a representative of the Divine Feminine?'

He knew where she was driving at.

'I know you think I'm one, right', she was unrelenting, 'that's why you drink me every chance you get?'

'What makes you think so?'

'I'm not dumb Chris', she was eager, excited, 'you're too tense until you get it. I don't mind, I only want to know what makes you think I'm one.'

'You're one, what?'

'You said so Chris', she squealed, 'you know, an Angel or whatever.'

He smiled, 'That's your name isn't it Baby.'

'Chris!!!'

'Okay okay', he relented, 'it doesn't matter if I think

you're one, you need to understand how to identify one.'

'Uh huh?'

'One way is with the stars which culminate at birth.'

'Any particular ones you have in mind Chris?'

'Sirius; which the Egyptians called Sothis.'

'The brightest star in the Night Sky, right?'

'Yes. According to Giorgio de SANTILLANA, the Coptic table of lunar stations takes lambda upsilon Scorpii; or the Tail of the Scorpion; as the precise opposite of Sirius.'

'What's the big deal?'

'Remember the Hermetic axiom, "As Above So Below". Both Sothis and Selket are mirror opposites in the sky on opposite sides of the celestial hemispheres. The Egyptian Goddess Sothis is identified with water and the healing properties of nectar as well as the Goddess Selket whose colour is red and breathes fire and venom and brings about death and destruction.'

'And these Goddesses are interchangeable?'

'Not exactly, but again, think mirror image: Nectar and Venom have the same building blocks.'

'So what does that have to do with me?'

He continued, 'Did you know you were born under the stars Acumen and Aculeus; also called lambda upsilon Scorpii?'

'Great', she said, 'so?'

'The star Acumen is responsible for illumination; insight or inner-vision', he continued, 'and Aculeus for leadership ability. But that's not all.'

'I'm listening.'

'Bernadette Brady says that the Kelts celebrated the Sun's entry into Scorpio with the Feast of Samhain, for it was on that night that the gateway between the otherworld and the world of living was open.'

She waited.

'Want to know something amusing?'

'Uh huh?'

'The stars are also known as the Fish-Hook ', he teased.

'C'mon Chris, that's not fair!'

'Okay Okay', he said, 'here's something more – the examples of your constellation are Vincent Van Gogh, Mozart, Marilyn Monroe and . . . '

'Wasn't Van Gogh Sick in the Head (SITH)?'

'Yes, but the Revenge of the SITH is sweet', he grinned, 'all gifted people are crazy for example Ernest HEMINGWAY, Jim MORRISON, Kurt COBAIN, Pablo PICASSO and Sigmund FREUD to name a few.'

'Anyone I can be proud of?'

'Jeanne D'ARC.'

'Wow!!!'She was happy, excited, 'Is this some kind of language?'

'Could be', he was pleased, 'MIT Professor Harald REICHE(1922-1994)called it The Language of Archaic Astronomy. And the goddess ascribed to Lambda upsilon Scorpii is described by the Egyptians as Selket.'

'And the nectar of immortality is the gift of the Goddess?'

'Yes.'

'How Chris?'

'Let me give you another example - scorpion venom is found in the scorpion's tail.'

'Good for it, so what Chris?'

'It's dangerous, but a neurotoxin is a two-bladed knife. Recent research reveals its varied uses.'

'Such as?'

'Treatment of brain tumour for instance.'

'Wow!'

'And an alternative to morphine.'

'So am I venomous, Chris?' She asked with a smile.

'No way sweetheart; but try and recall traditional images of Goddesses which show them crushing a scorpion or a snake; it indicates the quality of a Goddess to sift nectar from venom.'

'Oh.'

'In pre-Dynastic Egypt, ignorant masses worshiped the Bull while the priests worshipped Selket.'

Pre-Dynastic Egypt? She didn't know or cared, just wanted to know more about herself.

'Lambda upsilon Scorpii covers 1/27th the population of this planet; any other indicators of the Goddess?'

He was impressed. 'How did you . . .'

'C'mon,' she was impatient. 'This is the Lunar Zodiac.'

He was impressed, 'Yes, but some indicators of the Goddess are pretty weird.'

'Not as freakin' weird as what we've discussed till now, I'm sure', she said tartly. 'So what are they?'

'For one thing, Angels don't, uh huh, smell.'

'Thanx for telling me now, Chris,' she said, 'after I've spent a fortune in Listerine POCKETPAKS.'

'It's simple really,' he explained, 'the bodies of Angels have more alkaline than acid content; and bacteria feed on acid.'

'Acid means sugar, right?'

'Yep.'

'And Angels reject sugar?'

'Uh huh,' he was puzzled.

She could grasp what went on in his head, as well as the cause of his desperation. She smiled; men were not only stupid but dumb; they thought they could hide, but not from her, 'Don't you see the pattern Chris?'

'Pattern?'

Her tone was gentle, 'You're so predictable, Chris. Think of Elizabeth Gilbert's Eat-Pray-Love ; for you it's Eat-Kinky Sex-Trigger the Release of Nectar (or DMT; take your pick)-Drink.'

'I don't get it.'

She sighed, neither did Tom Hanks in Big, but that was not her story, 'Like you said Chris, if Angels reject Sugar, their lovers can have their fill, right?'

He finally understood, 'That's pretty good.'

She grinned, 'Any other? Indicators I mean?'

'They're the daughters of the Holy Mother.'

'That's obvious.'

'You can't tell them anything they don't already know.'

'Wish it'd work during the GMAT.'

'They are natural healers.'

'Big freakin' deal!!! It's not Med School.'

'Kids adore them.'

'Yes,' she smiled, 'I can vouch for that. What else?'

'I'd rather not say.'

'Chris, we've gone too far, you've got to trust me', she coaxed him, 'after all, it's about me.'

He paused, then, 'When they die, it's usually due to Cancer.'

She didn't react but analysed it objectively, 'Doesn't jell.'

He explained. 'Death cannot strike where they are present 'coz their touch brims with life, instead, it increases the formation of Cancer cells.'

'Isn't that a contradiction, Chris?'

'No,' his tone was somber, 'they choose when they have to go.'

'Go where?'

'To merge with the Holy Mother.'

She was silent for a long time.

4 - SHAPE SHIFTING GODDESS

She'd learnt a lot, in the past few hours, seriously, no kidding!!!

'Some last questions Chris, just to satisfy my curiosity.'

'Sure Baby.'

'First, why do you suck my tongue', so desperately, she wanted to add, didn't, it wasn't polite, instead, 'so hard?'

'Let's understand the anthropological context first. Felicitas GOODMAN says sticking out the tongue was a religious trance ritual amongst the pagans.'

'How?'

'The Pentecostal's believe it's a manifestation of The Holy Spirit, of Baptism, without which no one would enter the Kingdom of Heaven.'

Her mind wandered. She could relate it to being tongue-tied, especially when he was around.

'She also writes that in American Indian art, you see figures of protruding tongues', he explained, 'connect it to making love – it may look relaxing, but is physically taxing.'

She knew what THAT was at least!

'She also says that a number of Amerindian traditions, on the Northwest Coast, for instance, receive power from

Shekinah

the spirits by way of the protruding tongue.'

'So you suck my tongue to get my power', she giggled.

'No Baby', he smiled, nibbled her lips, 'I do it to connect.'

'Does something else also happen? Like you become an animal or something?'

'Uh huh, "The ability to change shape or to transform into another object or creature was common in Keltic Mythology ".But why do you ask Sweetheart? Did you feel it?'

'Yes,' she blushed, 'I feel so stupid.'

'Why Baby?'

She felt awful, 'I felt like I'd turned into a Pig.'

'That's terrific Baby,' he smiled, 'the Wild Boar is the Keltic symbol of fertility.'

'What a relief,' she said, pleased, 'I'll never crack jokes about a Porco again.'

He laughed.

'And Chris, you said connect', that word again, 'is that when one becomes a zombie?'

He was startled, 'A… Wha . .a. . a. . a . . t?' At times she surprised him, took time to think, 'you're right Baby, in a way, yes, it is a reflex action of nature; well Baby, there's some truth in that, you do become a zombie.'

'The first time', she said in a small voice, 'when you turned into one- you hurt me Chris.'

'I'm ever so sorry Baby', he recalled, 'I can't hurt you . . . without hurting myself.'

She was grateful for the admission, although by now she knew.

'Yes, I did become a Zombie', he continued, 'but that was because I was afraid of losing you, and also because I wanted you so bad, it hurt.'

'Why didn't you tell me?'

He didn't answer, his thoughts were faraway.

'Why Chris', she persisted, 'we wasted so much time.'

'Speaking of time', he nibbled her ear, 'check the clock.'

She was exasperated, she'd almost cornered him!!!Took a quick look at the clock - it was a quarter to 4 - then squealed with delight as he lifted her in his arms.

'I know Chris, I know', she sighed, 'it's time to clean-up."

5 - ASHERAH

Last shower before we split, her hands were busy with gel, she sensed something in the atmosphere, a tinge of sadness that it'd be over.

He nuzzled her, held her lightly, skin-on-skin, she felt light-headed, a sense of déjà vu, was this how it was meant to be?

Screw her hair, she soaked in the shower, turned her face to catch the needle jets, relaxed in the warm water, wondered about how she'd feel when he left.

It hit her then, almost like a physical blow, she bit her lip, caught her breath. Don't cry, she told herself, don't ruin it, for him, as well as for you, in these final moments of such a beautiful day. Her mind was numb, had drawn a blank, should she try to connect? Take a 'Trip Through the Water Door' like he'd said? She closed her eyes to pray - Stella Maris, Mother of God, help me.

'Try NOT to think, let it go.'

She understood who it was!!! 'NO!!!' She fought back, 'NO-NO-NO-NO-NO!!! It's NOT fair!!!'

'Life's NOT fair, My Child, there are many paths to tread, both of you are my children, I have different Work for you.'

'Why me, Mother, why me?' Tears of rage, hot, mingled with the shower, 'Why give me a glimpse of Heaven; then Death?'

'Did you NOT want this? Did I not give you what you wanted? Have I not come when called? Did I ever ask you if it was right?'

Shoulders slumped, 'No, Mother, you were always there . . . with me', there was nothing left to say; and yet, one last try.

'What about him? Will he survive', without me, she wanted to add, didn't or couldn't.

'Leave him to his destiny, to walk the road I've chosen for him. Don't spoil it now; there is God's Work to be done by both of you.'

She couldn't hold back any more, 'Please Mother, the pain.' She felt she'd split apart.

'Nothing compared to what my Son went through.'

She remembered, a calm descended over her, no, she wouldn't be sick, Think-Think-Think.

'Do not blame yourself My Child. It was I who brought you two together, and it is I who make you part: try and remember, this is not the first time; and it won't be the last.'

Yes, she knew now, but something else clicked as well, there were two things about Her - She never got mad; and She never said 'No.' She knew, then, what to do next, it'd be alright, she smiled - she'd won.

'But if I still want him, will you grant me that Mother?'

There was no answer, or was it a pause? She was suddenly frantic.

'Yes, My Child, you are my flesh and blood, my favourite.'

'Then bless me Mother.'

Shekinah

'Abençoo-vos com o conhecimento do Santo Mistério entre mulher e o homem a se unirem como uma só carne para cumprir o meu objetivo e ser dotado para sempre com Vida, Luz e o Amor '

She'd made it!!! Her body tingled, alive with excitement, 'Thank you Mother.' Quick, before She goes away, 'When will I see you again?'

'I am everywhere, in every cell of your body, in every particle of the Universe . . . but I appear only to those who love.'

And She was gone.

'Oooowwwwwwww . . . ,' he'd bit her hard, so much for the pain, she smiled, looked at her shoulders, saw crescent shaped bruises, they'd turn green, then blue, no Tees for a while, 'what Chris', she asked, her voice gentle, soft.

'A blank canvas, Baby', he grinned happily, 'couldn't resist.'

He saw the look on her face, misunderstood, 'Do we have time?'

She nodded, 'Take your time Chris', she put her hand gently behind his head, 'there's always time for love.'

CPSIA information can be obtained at www.ICGtesting.com
Printed in the USA
BVOW10s1804210615

405520BV00010B/93/P